„ "Every moment, Lord, I need
the merit of thy death."

JOHN WESLEY

Poems of Charles Wesley

1747
D1663494

CHARLES WESLEY

als DANKESCHÖN

Dennic

TABLE OF CONTENTS

PART I. A CHARGE TO KEEP I HAVE

A CHARGE TO KEEP I HAVE

A charge to keep I have,
A God to glorify,
A never-dying soul to save,
And fit it for the sky.

To serve the present age,
My calling to fulfill;
O may it all my powers engage
To do my Master's will!

Arm me with jealous care,
As in thy sight to live,
And oh, thy servant, Lord,
Prepare a strict account to give!

Help me to watch and pray,
And on thyself rely,
Assured, if I my trust betray,
I shall forever die.

AND AM I BORN TO DIE

And am I born to die?
To lay this body down?

And must my trembling spirit fly
Into a world unknown -
A land of deepest shade,
Unpierced by human thought,
The dreary regions of the dead,
Where all things are forgot?

Soon as from earth I go,
What will become of me?
Eternal happiness or woe
Must then my portion be;
Waked by the trumpet's sound,
I from my grave shall rise,
And see the Judge with glory crowned,
And see the flaming skies.

How shall I leave my tomb?
With triumph or regret?
A fearful or a joyful doom,
A curse or blessing meet?
Will angel-bands convey
Their brother to the bar?
Or devils drag my soul away,
To meet its sentence there?

Who can resolve the doubt
That tears my anxious breast?
Shall I be with the damned cast out,
Or numbered with the blest?
I must from God be driven,
Or with my Saviour dwell;
Must come at his command to heaven,
Or else - depart to hell.

O thou that wouldst not have
One wretched sinner die,
Who died'st thyself; my soul to save
From endless misery!
Show me the way to shun
Thy dreadful wrath severe,
That when thou comest on thy throne
I may with joy appear.

Thou art thyself the Way;
Thyself in me reveal;
So shall I spend my life's short day
Obedient to thy will;
So shall I love my God,
Because he first loved me,
And praise thee in thy bright abode,
To all eternity.

AND AM I ONLY BORN TO DIE

And am I only born to die?
And must I suddenly comply
With nature's stern decree?
What after death for me remains?
Celestial joys, or hellish pains,
To all eternity?

How then ought I on earth to live,
While God prolongs the kind reprieve
And props the house of clay?
My sole concern, my single care,
To watch, and tremble, and prepare
Against the fatal day.

No room for mirth or trifling here,
For worldly hope, or worldly fear,
If life so soon is gone:
If now the Judge is at the door,
And all mankind must stand before
The inexorable throne!

No matter which my thoughts employ,
A moment's misery, or joy;
But O! when both shall end,
Where shall I find my destined place?
Shall I my everlasting days
With fiends, or angels spend?

Nothing is worth a thought beneath
But how I may escape the death
That never, never dies;
How make mine own election sure,

And, when I fail on earth, secure
A mansion in the skies.

Jesus, vouchsafe a pitying ray,
Be Thou my guide, be Thou my way
To glorious happiness;
Ah, write the pardon on my heart,
And whensoe'er I hence depart,
Let me depart in peace.

AND ARE WE YET ALIVE

And are we yet alive,
And see each other's face?
Glory and thanks to Jesus give
For his almighty grace!

Preserved by power divine
To full salvation here,
Again in Jesus' praise we join,
And in his sight appear.

What troubles have we seen,
What mighty conflicts past,
Fightings without, and fears within,
Since we assembled last!

Yet out of all the Lord
Hath brought us by his love;
And still he doth his help afford,
And hides our life above.

Then let us make our boast
Of his redeeming power,
Which saves us to the uttermost,
Till we can sin no more.

Let us take up the cross
Till we the crown obtain,
And gladly reckon all things loss
So we may Jesus gain.

AND CAN I YET DELAY

And can I yet delay
My little all to give?
To tear my soul from earth away
For Jesus to receive?

Nay, but I yield, I yield;
I can hold out no more;
I sink, by dying love compelled,
And own Thee Conqueror.

Though late, I all forsake;
My friends, my all, resign;
Gracious Redeemer, take, O take,
And seal me ever Thine!

Come, and possess me whole,
Nor hence again remove;
Settle and fix my wavering soul
With all Thy weight of love.

AND CAN IT BE THAT I SHOULD GAIN

And can it be that I should gain
An interest in the Savior's blood!
Died he for me, who caused his pain!
For me? who him to death pursued?
Amazing love! How can it be
That thou, my God, shouldst die for me?
Amazing love! How can it be
That thou, my God, shouldst die for me?

'Tis mystery all: th' Immortal dies!
Who can explore his strange design?
In vain the firstborn seraph tries
To sound the depths of love divine.
'Tis mercy all! Let earth adore;
Let angel minds inquire no more.
'Tis mercy all! Let earth adore;
Let angel minds inquire no more.

He left his Father's throne above
So free, so infinite his grace!

Emptied himself of all but love,
And bled for Adam's helpless race.
'Tis mercy all, immense and free,
For O my God, it found out me!
'Tis mercy all, immense and free,
For O my God, it found out me!

Long my imprisoned spirit lay,
Fast bound in sin and nature's night;
Thine eye diffused a quickening ray;
I woke, the dungeon flamed with light;
My chains fell off, my heart was free,
I rose, went forth, and followed thee.
My chains fell off, my heart was free,
I rose, went forth, and followed thee.

Still the small inward voice I hear,
That whispers all my sins forgiven;
Still the atoning blood is near,
That quenched the wrath of hostile Heaven.
I feel the life His wounds impart;
I feel the Savior in my heart.
I feel the life His wounds impart;
I feel the Savior in my heart.

No condemnation now I dread;
Jesus, and all in him, is mine;
Alive in him, my living Head,
And clothed in righteousness divine,
Bold I approach th' eternal throne,
And claim the crown, through Christ my own.
Bold I approach th' eternal throne,
And claim the crown, through Christ my own.

AND LET OUR BODIES PART

And let our bodies part,
To different climes repair;
Inseparably joined in heart
The friends of Jesus are.

O let us still proceed
In Jesus' work below;

And, following our triumphant Head,
To further conquests go!

The vineyard of the Lord
Before His laborers lies;
And lo! we see the vast reward
Which waits us in the skies.

O let our heart and mind
Continually ascend,
That haven of repose to find,
Where all our labors end.

When all our toils are o'er,
Our suffering and our pain!
Who meet on that eternal shore
Shall never part again.

AND LET THIS FEEBLE BODY FAIL

And let this feeble body fail,
And let it droop and die;
My soul shall quit the mournful vale,
And soar to worlds on high;
Shall join the disembodied saints,
And find its long sought rest,
That only bliss for which it pants,
In my Redeemer's breast.

In hope of that immortal crown
I now the cross sustain,
And gladly wander up and down,
And smile at toil and pain:
I suffer out my threescore years,
Till my Deliverer come,
And wipe away His servant's tears,
And take His exile home.

O what hath Jesus bought for me!
Before my ravished eyes
Rivers of life divine I see,
And trees of paradise:
I see a world of spirits bright,

Who taste the pleasures there;
They all are robed in spotless white,
And conquering palms they bear.

O what are all my sufferings here,
If, Lord, Thou count me meet
With that enraptured host to appear,
And worship at Thy feet!
Give joy or grief, give ease or pain,
Take life or friends away,
But let me find them all again
In that eternal day.

AND MUST I BE TO JUDGMENT BROUGHT

And must I be to judgment brought,
And answer in that day,
For every vain and idle thought,
And every word I say?

Yes, every secret of my heart,
Shall shortly be made known,
And I receive my just desert
For all that I have done.

How careful, then ought I to live,
With what religious fear!
Who such a strict account must give
For my behavior here.

Thou awful Judge of quick and dead,
The watchful power bestow;
So shall I to my ways take heed,
To all I speak or do.

If now Thou standest at the door,
O let me feel Thee near,
And make my peace with God, before
I at Thy bar appear.

AND WILT THOU YET BE FOUND

And wilt Thou yet be found,

And may I still draw near?
Then listen to the plaintive sound
Of a poor sinner's prayer.

Jesus, thine aid afford,
If still the same thou art:
to thee I look, to thee, my Lord,
I lift my helpless heart.

Thou seest my troubled breast,
The strugglings of my will,
The foes that interrupt my rest,
The agonies I feel.

O my offended Lord,
Restore my inward peace;
I know thou canst; pronounce the word,
And bid the tempest cease.

I long to see thy face;
Thy Spirit I implore--
The living water of thy grace
That I may thirst no more.

ANGELS YOUR MARCH OPPOS

Angels your march oppose,
Who still in strength excel,
Your secret, sworn, eternal foes,
Countless, invisible.
With rage that never ends
Their hellish arts they try;
Legions of dire malicious fiends,
And spirits enthroned on high.

On earth the usurpers reign,
Exert their baneful power,
O'er the poor fallen sons of men
They tyrannize their hour:
But shall believers fear?
But shall believers fly?
Or see the bloody cross appear,
And all their power defy?

Jesus' tremendous Name
Puts all our foes to flight:
Jesus, the meek, the angry Lamb,
A Lion is in fight.
By all hell's host withstood,
We all hell's host o'erthrow;
And conquering them, through Jesus' blood,
We still to conquer go.

Our Captain leads us on;
He beckons from the skies,
And reaches out a starry crown,
And bids us take the prize:
"Be faithful unto death;
Partake My victory;
And thou shalt wear this glorious wreath.
And thou shalt reign with Me."

ARE THERE NOT IN THE LABOURER'S DAY

Are there not in the labourer's day
Twelve hours, in which he safely may
His calling's work pursue?
Though sin and Satan still are near,
Nor sin nor Satan can I fear,
With Jesus in my view.

Not all the powers of hell can fright
A soul that walks with Christ in light,
He walks and cannot fall;
Clearly he sees, and wins his way,
Shining unto the perfect day,
And more than conquers all.

Light of the world, thy beams I bless;
On thee, bright Sun of righteousness,
My faith hath fixed its eye;
Guided by thee, through all I go,
Nor fear the ruin spread below,
For thou art always nigh.

Ten thousand snares my path beset;

Yet will I, Lord, the work complete
Which thou to me hast given;
Regardless of the pains I feel,
Close by the gates of death and hell,
I urge my way to heaven.

Still will I strive, and labour still,
With humble zeal to do thy will,
And trust in thy defence:
My soul into thy hands I give;
And, if he can obtain thy leave,
Let Satan pluck me thence!

ARISE, MY SOUL, ARISE

Arise, my soul, arise; shake off thy guilty fears;
The bleeding sacrifice in my behalf appears:
Before the throne my surety stands,
Before the throne my surety stands,
My name is written on His hands.

He ever lives above, for me to intercede;
His all redeeming love, His precious blood, to plead:
His blood atoned for all our race,
His blood atoned for all our race,
And sprinkles now the throne of grace.

Five bleeding wounds He bears; received on Calvary;
They pour effectual prayers; they strongly plead for me:
"Forgive him, O forgive," they cry,
"Forgive him, O forgive," they cry,
"Nor let that ransomed sinner die!"

The Father hears Him pray, His dear anointed One;
He cannot turn away, the presence of His Son;
His Spirit answers to the blood,
His Spirit answers to the blood,
And tells me I am born of God.

My God is reconciled; His pardoning voice I hear;
He owns me for His child; I can no longer fear:
With confidence I now draw nigh,
With confidence I now draw nigh,

And "Father, Abba, Father," cry.

ARISE, MY SOUL, ON WINGS SUBLIME

Arise, my soul, on wings sublime,
Above the vanities of time;
Let faith now pierce the veil, and see
The glories of eternity.

Born by a new, celestial birth,
Why should I grovel here on earth?
Why grasp at vain and fleeting toys,
So near to heaven's eternal joys?

Shall aught beguile me on the road,
The narrow road that leads to God?
Or can I love this earth so well,
As not to long with God to dwell?

To dwell with God, to taste his love,
Is the full heaven enjoyed above:
The glorious expectation now
Is heavenly bliss begun below.

ARM OF THE LORD, AWAKE, AWAKE

Arm of the Lord, awake, awake!
Thine own immortal strength put on!
With terror clothed, hell's kingdom shake,
And cast Thy foes with fury down!

As in the ancient days appear!
The sacred annals speak Thy fame:
Be now omnipotently near,
To endless ages still the same.

Thy arm, Lord, is not shortened now,
It wants not now the power to save;
Still present with Thy people, Thou
Bear'st them through life's disparted wave.

By death and hell pursued in vain,
To Thee the ransomed seed shall come,

Shouting their heavenly Zion gain,
And pass through death triumphant home.

The pain of life shall there be o'er,
The anguish and distracting care,
There sighing grief shall weep no more,
And sin shall never enter there.

Where pure, essential joy is found,
The Lord's redeemed their heads shall raise,
With everlasting gladness crowned,
And filled with love, and lost in praise.

AUTHOR OF FAITH, ETERNAL WORD

Author of faith, eternal Word,
Whose Spirit breathes the active flame;
Faith like its finisher and Lord,
Today as yesterday the same.

To Thee our humble hearts aspire,
And ask the gift unspeakable;
Increase in us the kindled fire,
In us the work of faith fulfill.

By faith we know Thee strong to save;
Save us, a present Savior Thou!
Whate'er we hope, by faith we have
Future and past subsisting now.

To him that in Thy Name believes
Eternal life with Thee is given;
Into Himself He all receives,
Pardon and holiness, and Heaven.

The things unknown to feeble sense,
Unseen by reason's glimmering ray,
With strong commanding evidence
Their heavenly origin display.

Faith lends its realizing light,
The clouds disperse, the shadows fly;
Th'invisible appears in sight,

And God is seen by mortal eye.

AUTHOR OF FAITH, TO THEE I CRY

Author of faith, to thee I cry,
To thee, who wouldst not have me die,
But know the truth and live;
Open mine eyes to see thy face,
Work in my heart the saving grace,
The life eternal give.

Shut up in unbelief I groan,
And blindly serve a God unknown,
Till thou the veil remove;
The gift unspeakable impart,
And write thy name upon my heart,
And manifest thy love.

I know the work is only thine,
The gift of faith is all divine;
But, if on thee we call,
Thou wilt the benefit bestow,
And give us hearts to feel and know
That thou hast died for all.

Thou bidd'st us knock and enter in,
Come unto thee, and rest from sin,
The blessing seek and find;
Thou bidd'st us ask thy grace, and have;
Thou canst, thou wouldst, this moment save
Both me and all mankind.

Be it according to thy word!
Now let me find my pardoning Lord,
Let what I ask be given;
The bar of unbelief remove,
Open the door of faith and love,
And take me into heaven.

AUTHOR OF FAITH, WE SEEK THY FACE

Author of faith, we seek thy face
For all who feel thy work begun;

Confirm and strengthen them in grace,
And bring thy feeblest children on.

Thou seest their wants, thou know'st their names,
Be mindful of thy youngest care;
Be tender of thy new-born lambs,
And gently in thy bosom bear.

The lion roaring for his prey,
And ravening wolves on every side,
Watch over them to tear and slay,
If found one moment from their guide.

Satan his thousand arts essays,
His agents all their powers employ,
To blast the blooming work of grace,
The heavenly offspring to destroy.

Baffle the crooked serpent's skill,
And turn his sharpest dart aside;
Hide from their eyes the devilish ill,
O save them from the demon, pride!

In safety lead thy little flock,
From hell, the world, and sin secure;
And set their feet upon the rock,
And make in thee their goings sure.

AUTHOR OF OUR SALVATION, THEE

Author of our salvation, thee,
With lowly, thankful hearts, we praise;
Author of this great mystery,
Figure and means of saving grace.

The sacred, true, effectual sign,
Thy body and thy blood it shows;
The glorious instrument divine,
Thy mercy and thy strength bestows.

We see the blood that seals our peace;
Thy pardoning mercy we receive;
The bread doth visibly express

The strength through which our spirits live.

Our spirits drink a fresh supply,
And eat the bread so freely given,
Till, borne on eagle wings, we fly,
And banquet with our Lord in heaven.

AWAKE, JERUSALEM, AWAKE

Awake, Jerusalem, awake!
No longer in thy sins lie down;
The garment of salvation take,
Thy beauty and thy strength put on.

Shake off the dust that blinds thy sight,
And hides the promise from thine eyes;
Arise, and struggle into light,
The great Deliverer calls: Arise!

Shake off the bands of sad despair;
Zion, assert thy liberty;
Look up, thy broken heart prepare,
And God shall set the captive free.

Vessels of mercy, sons of grace,
Be purge from every sinful stain,
Be like your Lord, His Word embrace,
Nor bear His hallowed Name in vain.t

PART II. AWAY WITH OUR SORROW AND FEAR

AWAY WITH OUR SORROW AND FEAR

Away with our sorrow and fear!
We soon shall recover our home,
The city of saints shall appear,
The day of eternity come:
From earth we shall quickly remove,
And mount to our native abode,
The house of our Father above,
The palace of angels and God.

Our mourning is all at an end,
When, raised by the life-giving Word,
We see the new city descend,
Adorned as a bride for her Lord;
The city so holy and clean,
No sorrow can breathe in the air;
No gloom of affliction or sin,
No shadow of evil is there.

By faith we already behold
That lovely Jerusalem here;
Her walls are of jasper and gold,
As crystal her buildings are clear;
Immovably founded in grace,
She stands as she ever hath stood,
And brightly her Builder displays,
And flames with the glory of God.

No need of the sun in that day,
Which never is followed by night,
Where Jesus' beauties display
A pure and a permanent light:
The Lamb is their light and their sun,
And lo! by reflection they shine,
With Jesus ineffably one,
And bright in effulgence divine!

The saints in His presence receive
Their great and eternal reward;
In Jesus, in Heaven they live,
They reign in the smile of their Lord:
The flame of angelical love
Is kindled at Jesus' face;
And all the enjoyment above
Consists in the rapturous gaze.

AWAY, MY NEEDLESS FEARS

Away my needless fears,
And doubts no longer mine;
A ray of heavenly light appears,
A messenger divine.

Thrice comfortable hope,
That calms my troubled breast;
My Father's hand prepares the cup,
And what he wills is best.

If what I wish is good,
And suits the will divine;
By earth and hell in vain withstood,
I know it shall be mine.

Still let them counsel take
To frustrate his decree,
They cannot keep a blessing back
By heaven designed for me.

Here then I doubt no more,
But in his pleasure rest,

Whose wisdom, love, and truth, and power,
Engage to make me blest.

To accomplish his design
The creatures all agree;
And all the attributes divine
Are now at work for me.

BECAUSE THOU HAST SAID

Because Thou hast said, "Do this for My sake,"
The mystical bread we gladly partake;
We thirst for the Spirit that flows from above,
And long to inherit Thy fullness of love.

'Tis here we look up and grasp at Thy mind,
'Tis here that we hope Thine image to find;
The means of bestowing Thy gifts we embrace;
But all things are owing to Jesus' grace.

BEING OF BEINGS

Being of beings, God of love;
To Thee our hearts we raise;
Thy all sustaining power we prove,
And gladly sing Thy praise.

Thine, wholly Thine, we pant to be;
Our sacrifice receive;
Made, and preserved, and saved by Thee,
To Thee ourselves we give.

Heav'nward our every wish aspires,
For all Thy mercy's store;
The sole return Thy love requires,
Is that we ask for more.

For more we ask: we open then
Our hearts to embrace Thy will;
Turn and revive us, Lord, again,
With all Thy fullness fill.

Come, Holy Ghost, the Savior's love

Shed in our hearts abroad;
So shall we ever live, and move,
And be, with Christ, in God.

BLEST BE THE DEAR UNITING LOVE

Blest be the dear uniting love
That will not let us part;
Our bodies may far off remove,
We still are one in heart.

Joined in one spirit to our Head,
Where he appoints we go,
And still in Jesus' footsteps tread,
And do his work below.

O may we ever walk in him,
And nothing know beside,
Nothing desire, nothing esteem,
But Jesus crucified!

Closer and closer let us cleave
To His beloved embrace;
Expect His fullness to receive
And grace to answer grace.

While thus we walk with Christ in light
Who shall our souls disjoin,
Souls, which Himself vouchsafes t'unite
In fellowship divine!

We all are one who him receive,
And each with each agree,
In him the One, the Truth, we live;
Blest point of unity!

Partakers of the Savior's grace,
The same in mind and heart,
Nor joy, nor grief, nor time, nor place,
Nor life, nor death can part.

But let us hasten to the day
Which shall our flesh restore,

When death shall all be done away,
And bodies part no more!

BLOW YE THE TRUMPET, BLOW

Blow ye the trumpet, blow!
The gladly solemn sound
Let all the nations know,
To earth's remotest bound:

Refrain:
The year of jubilee is come!
The year of jubilee is come!
Return, ye ransomed sinners, home.

Jesus, our great high priest,
Hath full atonement made;
Ye weary spirits, rest;
Ye mournful souls, be glad:
(Refrain)

Extol the Lamb of God,
The all atoning Lamb;
Redemption in his blood
Throughout the world proclaim.
(Refrain)

Ye slaves of sin and hell,
Your liberty receive,
And safe in Jesus dwell,
And blest in Jesus live:
(Refrain)

Ye who have sold for nought
Your heritage above
Shall have it back unbought,
The gift of Jesus' love:
(Refrain)

The gospel trumpet hear,
The news of heavenly grace;
And saved from earth, appear
Before your Savior's face:

(Refrain)

BY FAITH WE FIND THE PLACE ABOVE

By faith we find the place above,
The Rock that rent in twain;
Beneath the shade of divine love,
And in the clefts remain.

Jesus, to Thy dear wounds we flee,
We sink into Thy side;
Assured that all who trust in Thee
Shall evermore abide.

Then let the thundering trumpet sound,
The latest lightning glare,
The mountains melt, the solid ground
Dissolve as liquid air.

The huge celestial bodies roll,
Amidst that general fire,
And shrivel as a parchment scroll,
And all in smoke expire!

Yet still the Lord, the Savior reigns,
When nature is destroyed,
And no created thing remains
Throughout the flaming void.

Sublime upon His azure throne,
He speaks the almighty word;
His fiat is obeyed! 'tis done;
And Paradise restored.

So be it! let this system end,
This ruinous earth and skies,
The new Jerusalem descend,
The new creation rise!

Thy power omnipotent assume,
Thy brightest majesty!
And when Thou dost in glory come,
My Lord, remember me!

CAPTAIN OF ISRAEL'S HOST

Captain of Israel's host, and Guide
Of all who seek the land above,
Beneath Thy shadow we abide,
The cloud of Thy protecting love;
Our strength, Thy grace; our rule, Thy Word;
Our end, the glory of the Lord.

By Thine unerring Spirit led,
We shall not in the desert stray;
The light of man's direction need
Or miss our providential way;
As far from danger as from fear,
While Love, almighty Love, is near.

CELEBRATE IMMANUEL'S NAME

Celebrate Immanuel's Name, the Prince of life and peace.
God with us, our lips proclaim, our faithful hearts confess.
God is in our flesh revealed; Heav'n and earth in Jesus join.
Mortal with Immortal filled, and human with Divine.

Fullness of the Deity in Jesus' body dwells,
Dwells in all His saints and me when God His Son reveals.
Father, manifest Thy Son; breathe the true incarnate Word.
In our inmost souls make known the presence of the Lord.

Let the Spirit of our Head through every member flow;
By our Lord inhabited, we then Immanuel know.
Then He doth His Name express; God in us we truly prove,
Find with all the life of grace and all the power of love.

CHRIST THE LORD IS RISEN TODAY

Christ the Lord is risen today, Alleluia!
Sons of men and angels say, Alleluia!
Raise your joys and triumphs high, Alleluia!
Sing, ye heavens, and earth reply, Alleluia!

Love's redeeming work is done, Alleluia!
Fought the fight, the battle won, Alleluia!

Death in vain forbids him rise, Alleluia!
Christ has opened paradise, Alleluia!

Vain the stone, the watch, the seal, Alleluia!
Christ hath burst the gates of hell, Alleluia!
Death in vain forbids His rise, Alleluia!
Christ hath opened paradise, Alleluia!

Lives again our glorious King, Alleluia!
Where, O death, is now thy sting? Alleluia!
Once he died our souls to save, Alleluia!
Where's thy victory, boasting grave? Alleluia!

Soar we now where Christ has led, Alleluia!
Following our exalted Head, Alleluia!
Made like him, like him we rise, Alleluia!
Ours the cross, the grave, the skies, Alleluia!

Hail, the Lord of earth and heaven, Alleluia!
Praise to Thee by both be given, Alleluia!
Thee we greet triumphant now, Alleluia!
Hail, the resurrection day, Alleluia!

King of glory, Soul of bliss, Alleluia!
Everlasting life is this, Alleluia!
Thee to know, Thy power to prove, Alleluia!
Thus to sing and thus to love, Alleluia!

Hymns of praise then let us sing, Alleluia!
Unto Christ, our heavenly King, Alleluia!
Who endured the cross and grave, Alleluia!
Sinners to redeem and save. Alleluia!

But the pains that He endured, Alleluia!
Our salvation have procured, Alleluia!
Now above the sky He's King, Alleluia!
Where the angels ever sing. Alleluia!

Jesus Christ is risen today, Alleluia!
Our triumphant holy day, Alleluia!
Who did once upon the cross, Alleluia!
Suffer to redeem our loss. Alleluia!

CHRIST, FROM WHOM ALL BLESSINGS FLOW

Christ, from whom all blessings flow,
Perfecting the saints below,
Hear us, who thy nature share,
Who thy mystic body are.

Join us, in one spirit join,
Let us still receive of thine;
Still for more on thee we call,
Thou who fillest all in all.

Move and actuate and guide,
Diverse gifts to each divide;
Placed according to thy will,
Let us all our work fulfill;

Sweetly may we all agree,
Touched with loving sympathy,
Kindly for each other care;
Every member feel its share.

Never from thy service move,
Needful to each other prove;
Use the grace on each bestowed,
Tempered by the art of God.

Many are we now, and one,
We who Jesus have put on;
There is neither bond nor free,
Male nor female, Lord, in thee.

Love, like death, hath all destroyed,
Rendered all distinctions void;
Names and sects and parties fall;
Thou, O Christ, art all in all!

CHRIST, WHOSE GLORY FILLS THE SKIES

Christ, whose glory fills the skies,
Christ, the true, the only light,
Sun of Righteousness, arise,
Triumph o'er the shades of night;

Dayspring from on high, be near;
Daystar, in my heart appear.

Dark and cheerless is the morn
Unaccompanied by thee;
Joyless is the day's return,
Till thy mercy's beams I see;
Till they inward light impart,
Glad my eyes and warm my heart.

Visit then this soul of mine;
Pierce the gloom of sin and grief;
Fill me, Radiancy divine,
Scatter all my unbelief;
More and more thyself display,
Shining to the perfect day.

CLAP YOUR HANDS, YE PEOPLE ALL

Clap your hands, ye people all,
Praise the God on Whom ye call;
Lift your voice, and shout His praise,
Triumph in His sovereign grace!

Glorious is the Lord most High,
Terrible in majesty;
He His sovereign sway maintains,
King o'er all the earth He reigns.

Jesus is gone up on high,
Takes His seat above the sky:
Shout the angel-choirs aloud,
Echoing to the trump of God.

Sons of earth, the triumph join,
Praise Him with the host divine;
Emulate the heavenly powers,
Their victorious Lord is ours.

Shout the God enthroned above,
Trumpet forth His conquering love;
Praises to our Jesus sing,
Praises to our glorious King!

Power is all to Jesus given,
Power o'er hell, and earth, and Heav'n!
Power He now to us imparts;
Praise Him with believing hearts.

Wonderful in saving power,
Him let all our hearts adore;
Earth and Heav'n repeat the cry,
"Glory be to God most High!"

COME AWAY TO THE SKIES

Come away to the skies, my belovèd, arise
And rejoice in the day thou wast born;
On this festival day, come exulting away,
And with singing to Zion return.

We have laid up our love and our treasure above,
Though our bodies continue below.
The redeemed of the Lord will remember His Word,
And with singing to paradise go.

Now with singing and praise let us spend all the days
By our heavenly Father bestowed,
While His grace we receive from His bounty, and live
To the honor and glory of God!

For the glory we were first created to share,
Both the nature and kingdom divine,
Now created again that our lives may remain
Throughout time and eternity Thine.

We with thanks do approve the design
Of that love that hath joined us to Jesus' Name;
Now united in heart, let us never more part,
Till we meet at the feast of the Lamb.

There, Oh! there at His feet, we shall all likewise meet,
And be parted in body no more;
We shall sing to our lyres, with the heavenly choirs,
And our Savior in glory adore.

Hallelujah! we sing to our Father and King,
And His rapturous praises repeat:
To the Lamb that was slain, Hallelujah again!
Sing all Heaven and fall at His feet!

COME, AND LET US SWEETLY JOIN

Come and let us sweetly join,
Christ to praise in hymns divine;
Give we all with one accord
Glory to our common Lord.

Sing we then in Jesus' Name,
Now as yesterday the same;
One in every time and place,
Full for all of truth and grace.

We for Christ, our Master, stand,
Lights in a benighted land:
We our dying Lord confess;
We are Jesus' witnesses.

Witnesses that Christ hath died,
We with Him are crucified;
Christ hath burst the bands of death,
We His quickening Spirit breathe.

Strive we, in affection strive;
Let the purer flame revive,
Such as in the martyrs glowed,
Dying champions for their God.

Make us all in Thee complete,
Make us all for glory meet,
Meet to appear before Thy sight,
Partners with the saints in light.

We, like them, may live and love;
Called we are their joys to prove,
Saved with them from future wrath,
Partners of like precious faith.

Let the fruits of grace abound;

Let in us Thy vowels sound;
Faith, and love, and joy increase,
Temperance and gentleness.

Plant in us Thy humble mind;
Patient, pitiful, and kind,
Meek and lowly let us be,
Full of goodness, full of Thee.

Christ is now gone up on high,
Where to Him our wishes fly;
Sits at God's right hand above;
There with Him we reign in love!

Come, Thou high and lofty Lord!
Lowly, meek, incarnate Word!
Humbly stoop to earth again,
Come and visit abject men!

Hands and hearts and voices raise,
Sing as in the ancient days;
Antedate the joys above,
Celebrate the feast of love.

Jesus, dear expected guest,
Thou art bidden to the feast,
For Thyself our hearts prepare,
Come, and sit, and banquet there!

Jesus, we Thy promise claim,
We are met in Thy great Name;
In the midst do Thou appear,
Manifest Thy presence here!

Sanctify us, Lord, and bless,
Breathe Thy Spirit, give Thy peace,
Thou Thyself within us move,
Make our feast a feast of love.

Call, O call us each by name,
To the marriage of the Lamb;
Let us lean upon Thy breast,
Love be there our endless feast!

Let us join, ('tis God commands)
Let us join our hearts and hands
Help to gain our calling's hope,
Build we each the other up.

God His blessings shall dispense,
God shall crown His ordinance;
Meet in His appointed ways;
Nourish us with social grace.

Let us then as brethren love,
Faithfully His gifts improve,
Carry on the earnest strife,
Walk in holiness of life.

Still forget the things behind,
Follow Christ in heart and mind,
Toward the mark unwearied press,
Seize the crown of righteousness.

Plead we thus for faith alone,
Faith which by our works is shown:
God it is Who justifies;
Only faith the grace applies.

Active faith that lives within,
Conquers earth, and hell, and sin,
Sanctifies, and makes us whole,
Forms the Savior in the soul.

Let us for this faith contend,
Sure salvation is its end:
Heaven already is begun,
Everlasting life is won.

Only let us persevere,
Till we see our Lord appear,
Never from the Rock remove,
Saved by faith, which works by love.

Partners of a glorious hope,
Lift your hearts and voices up,

Jointly let us rise, and sing
Christ our Prophet, Priest, and King.

Monuments of Jesus' grace,
Speak we by our lives His praise;
Walk in Him we have received,
Show we not in vain believed.

While we walk with God in light,
God our hearts doth still unite;
Dearest fellowship we prove,
Fellowship in Jesus' love.

Sweetly each, with each combined,
In the bonds of duty joined,
Feels the cleansing blood applied,
Daily feels that Christ hath died.

Still, O Lord, our faith increase,
Cleanse from all unrighteousness,
Thee the unholy cannot see;
Make, O make us meet for Thee!

Every vile affection kill,
Root out every seed of ill,
Utterly abolish sin,
Write Thy law of love within.

Hence may all our actions flow,
Love the proof that Christ we know;
Mutual love the token be,
Lord, that we belong to Thee

Love, Thine image, love impart!
Stamp it on our face and heart!
Only love to us be given!
Lord, we ask no other heaven.

COME, DIVINE INTERPRETER

Come, divine Interpreter,
Bring me eyes Thy book to read,
Ears the mystic words to hear,

Words which did from Thee proceed,
Words that endless bliss impart,
Kept in an obedient heart.

All who read, or hear, are blessed,
If Thy plain commands we do;
Of Thy kingdom here possessed,
Thee we shall in glory view
When Thou comest on earth to abide,
Reign triumphant at Thy side.

COME, FATHER, SON, AND HOLY GHOST

Come, Father, Son, and Holy Ghost,
Whom one all-perfect God we own,
Restorer of Thine image lost,
Thy various offices make known;
Display, our fallen souls to raise,
Thy whole economy of grace.

Jehovah in Three Persons, come,
And draw, and sprinkle us, and seal
Poor, guilty, dying worms, in whom
Thou dost eternal life reveal;
The knowledge of Thyself bestow,
And all Thy glorious goodness show.

Soon as our pardoned hearts believe
That Thou art pure, essential love,
The proof we in ourselves receive
Of the three witnesses above;
Sure, as the saints around Thy throne,
That Father, Word, and Spirit, are One.

O that we now, in love renewed,
Might blameless in Thy sight appear:
Wake we in Thy similitude,
Stamped with the Triune character;
Flesh, spirit, soul, to Thee resign,
And live and die entirely Thine!

COME, HOLY GHOST, OUR HEARTS INSPIRE

Come, Holy Ghost, our hearts inspire,
Let us thine influence prove;
Source of the old prophetic fire,
Fountain of life and love.

Come, Holy Ghost (for moved by thee
The prophets wrote and spoke),
Unlock the truth, thyself the key,
Unseal the sacred book.

Expand thy wings, celestial Dove,
Brood o'er our nature's night;
On our disordered spirits move,
And let there now be light.

God, through the Spirit we shall know
If thou within us shine,
And sound, with all thy saints below,
The depths of love divine.

COME, LET US ANEW OUR JOURNEY PURSUE

Come, let us anew our journey pursue,
Roll round with the year,
And never stand still till the Master appear,
His adorable will let us gladly fulfill,
And our talents improve,
By the patience of hope, and the labor of love,
By the patience of hope, and the labor of love.

Our life is a dream; our time, as a stream,
Glides swiftly away,
And the fugitive moment refuses to stay,
The arrow is flown, the moment is gone;
The millennial year
Rushes on to our view, and eternity's here,
Rushes on to our view, and eternity's here.

O that each in the day of His coming may say,
"I have fought my way through;
I have finished the work Thou didst give me to do!"
O that each from his Lord may receive the glad word,
"Well and faithfully done!

Enter into My joy, and sit down on My throne!"
"Enter into My joy, and sit down on My throne!"

COME, LET US JOIN OUR FRIENDS ABOVE

Come, let us join our friends above who have obtained the prize,
And on the eagle wings of love to joys celestial rise.
Let saints on earth unite to sing with those to glory gone,
For all the servants of our King in earth and heaven are one.

One family we dwell in him, one church above, beneath,
Though now divided by the stream, the narrow stream of death;
One army of the living God, to his command we bow;
Part of his host have crossed the flood, and part are crossing now.

Ten thousand to their endless home this solemn moment fly,
And we are to the margin come, and we expect to die.
His militant embodied host, with wishful looks we stand,
And long to see that happy coast, and reach the heavenly land.

Our old companions in distress we haste again to see,
And eager long for our release, and full felicity:
E'en now by faith we join our hands with those that went before,
And greet the blood-besprinkled bands on the eternal shore.

Our spirits too shall quickly join, like theirs with glory crowned,
And shout to see our Captain's sign, to hear this trumpet sound.
O that we now might grasp our Guide! O that the word were given!
Come, Lord of Hosts, the waves divide, and land us all in heaven.

PART III. COME, LET US RISE WITH CHRIST

COME, LET US RISE WITH CHRIST

Come, let us rise with Christ our Head
And seek the things above,
By the almighty Spirit led
And filled with faith and love;
Our hearts detached from all below
Should after Him ascend,
And only wish the joy to know
Of our triumphant Friend.

Enthroned at God's right hand He sits,
Maintainer of our cause,
Till every vanquished foe submits
To His victorious cross;
Worthy to be exalted thus,
The Lamb for sinners slain,
The Lord our King, Who reigns for us,
And shall forever reign.

To Him our willing hearts we give
Who gives us power and peace,
And dead to sin, His members live
The life of righteousness;
The hidden life of Christ is ours
With Christ concealed above,
And tasting the celestial powers,
We banquet on His love.

COME, LET US USE THE GRACE DIVINE

Come, let us use the grace divine, and all with one accord,
In a perpetual covenant join ourselves to Christ the Lord;
Give up ourselves, thru Jesus' power, his name to glorify;
And promise, in this sacred hour, for God to live and die.

The covenant we this moment make be ever kept in mind;
We will no more our God forsake, or cast these words behind.
We never will throw off the fear of God who hears our vow;
And if thou art well pleased to hear, come down and meet us now.

Thee, Father, Son, and Holy Ghost, let all our hearts receive,
Present with thy celestial host the peaceful answer give;
To each covenant the blood apply which takes our sins away,
And register our names on high and keep us to that day!

COME, LET US WHO IN CHRIST BELIEVE

Come, let us, who in Christ believe,
Our common Savior praise,
To Him with joyful voices give
The glory of His grace.

He now stands knocking at the door
Of every sinner's heart;
The worst need keep Him out no more,
Or force Him to depart.

Through grace we hearken to Thy voice,
Yield to be saved from sin;
In sure and certain hope rejoice,
That Thou wilt enter in.

Come quickly in, Thou heavenly Guest,
Nor ever hence remove;
But sup with us, and let the feast
Be everlasting love

COME, O THOU ALL VICTORIOUS LORD

Come, O Thou all-victorious Lord!

Thy power to us make known;
Strike with the hammer of Thy Word,
And break these hearts of stone.

O that we all might now begin
Our foolishness to mourn;
And turn at once from every sin,
And to our Savior turn!

Give us ourselves and Thee to know,
In this our gracious day;
Repentance unto life bestow,
And take our sins away.

Conclude us first in unbelief,
And freely then release;
Fill every soul with sacred grief,
And then with sacred peace.

Impoverish, Lord, and then relieve,
And then enrich the poor;
The knowledge of our sickness give,
The knowledge of our cure.

That blessèd sense of guilt impart,
And then remove the load;
Trouble, and wash the troubled heart
In the atoning blood.

Our desperate state through sin declare,
And speak our sins forgiv'n;
By perfect holiness prepare,
And take us up to Heav'n.

COME, O THOU TRAVELLER UNKNOWN

Come, O thou Traveller unknown,
Whom still I hold, but cannot see!
My company before is gone,
And I am left alone with Thee;
With Thee all night I mean to stay,
And wrestle till the break of day.

I need not tell Thee who I am,
My misery and sin declare;
Thyself hast called me by my name,
Look on Thy hands, and read it there;
But who, I ask Thee, who art Thou?
Tell me Thy name, and tell me now.

In vain Thou strugglest to get free,
I never will unloose my hold!
Art Thou the Man that died for me?
The secret of Thy love unfold;
Wrestling, I will not let Thee go,
Till I Thy name, Thy nature know.

Wilt Thou not yet to me reveal
Thy new, unutterable Name?
Tell me, I still beseech Thee, tell;
To know it now resolved I am;
Wrestling, I will not let Thee go,
Till I Thy Name, Thy nature know.

'Tis all in vain to hold Thy tongue
Or touch the hollow of my thigh;
Though every sinew be unstrung,
Out of my arms Thou shalt not fly;
Wrestling I will not let Thee go
Till I Thy name, Thy nature know.

What though my shrinking flesh complain,
And murmur to contend so long?
I rise superior to my pain,
When I am weak, then I am strong
And when my all of strength shall fail,
I shall with the God-man prevail.

Contented now upon my thigh
I halt, till life's short journey end;
All helplessness, all weakness I
On Thee alone for strength depend;
Nor have I power from Thee to move:
Thy nature, and Thy name is Love.

My strength is gone, my nature dies,

I sink beneath Thy weighty hand,
Faint to revive, and fall to rise;
I fall, and yet by faith I stand;
I stand and will not let Thee go
Till I Thy Name, Thy nature know.

Yield to me now, for I am weak,
But confident in self-despair;
Speak to my heart, in blessings speak,
Be conquered by my instant prayer;
Speak, or Thou never hence shalt move,
And tell me if Thy Name is Love.

'Tis Love! 'tis Love! Thou diedst for me!
I hear Thy whisper in my heart;
The morning breaks, the shadows flee,
Pure, universal love Thou art;
To me, to all, Thy bowels move;
Thy nature and Thy Name is Love.

My prayer hath power with God; the grace
Unspeakable I now receive;
Through faith I see Thee face to face,
I see Thee face to face, and live!
In vain I have not wept and strove;
Thy nature and Thy Name is Love.

I know Thee, Saviour, who Thou art.
Jesus, the feeble sinner's friend;
Nor wilt Thou with the night depart.
But stay and love me to the end,
Thy mercies never shall remove;
Thy nature and Thy Name is Love.

The Sun of righteousness on me
Hath rose with healing in His wings,
Withered my nature's strength; from Thee
My soul its life and succour brings;
My help is all laid up above;
Thy nature and Thy Name is Love.

Lame as I am, I take the prey,
Hell, earth, and sin, with ease o'ercome;

I leap for joy, pursue my way,
And as a bounding hart fly home,
Through all eternity to prove
Thy nature and Thy Name is Love.

COME, SINNERS, TO THE GOSPEL FEAST

Come, sinners, to the gospel feast,
let every soul be Jesus' guest.
Ye need not one be left behind,
for God hath bid all humankind.

Do not begin to make excuse;
ah! do not you his grace refuse;
your worldly cares and pleasures
leave, and take what Jesus hath to give.

Come and partake the gospel feast,
be saved from sin, in Jesus rest;
O taste the goodness of our God,
and eat his flesh and drink his blood.

See him set forth before your eyes;
behold the bleeding sacrifice;
his offered love make haste to embrace,
and freely now be saved by grace.

Ye who believe his record true
shall sup with him and he with you;
come to the feast, be saved from sin,
for Jesus waits to take you in.

COME, SINNERS, TO THE GOSPEL FEAST

Come, sinners, to the Gospel feast;
Let every soul be Jesus' guest.
Ye need not one be left behind,
For God hath bid all humankind.

Sent by my Lord, on you I call;
The invitation is to all.
Come, all the world! Come, sinner, thou!
All things in Christ are ready now.

Come, all ye souls by sin oppressed,
Ye restless wanderers after rest;
Ye poor, and maimed, and sick, and blind,
In Christ a hearty welcome find.

Come, and partake the Gospel feast;
Be saved from sin; in Jesus rest;
O taste the goodness of your God,
And eat His flesh, and drink His blood!

You vagrant souls, on you I call;
(O that my voice could reach you all!)
You all may now be justified,
You all may live, for Christ hath died.

My message as from God receive;
Ye all may come to Christ and live.
O let His love your hearts constrain,
Nor permit Him to die in vain.

His love is mighty to compel;
His conquering love consent to feel,
Yield to His love's resistless power,
And fight against your God no more.

See Him set forth before your eyes,
That precious, bleeding Sacrifice!
His offered benefits embrace,
And freely now be saved by grace.

This is the time, no more delay!
This is the Lord's accepted day.
Come thou, this moment, at His call,
And live for Him Who died for all.

COME, THOU ALMIGHTY KING

Come, Thou almighty King,
Help us Thy Name to sing, help us to praise!
Father all glorious, over all victorious,
Come and reign over us, Ancient of Days!

Jesus, our Lord, arise,
Scatter our enemies, and make them fall;
Let Thine almighty aid our sure defense be made,
Souls on Thee be stayed; Lord, hear our call.

Come, Thou incarnate Word,
Gird on Thy mighty sword, our prayer attend!
Come, and Thy people bless, and give Thy Word success,
Spirit of holiness, on us descend!

Come, holy Comforter,
Thy sacred witness bear in this glad hour.
Thou Who almighty art, now rule in every heart,
And ne'er from us depart, Spirit of power!

To Thee, great One in Three,
Eternal praises be, hence, evermore.
Thy sovereign majesty may we in glory see,
And to eternity love and adore!

COME, THOU CONQUEROR OF THE NATIONS

Come, Thou Conqueror of the nations,
Now on Thy white horse appear;
Earthquakes, famines, desolations
Signify Thy kingdom near:
True and faithful!
Stablish Thy dominion here.

Thine the kingdom, power, and glory;
Thine the ransomed nations are.
Let the heathen fall before Thee,
Let the isles Thy power declare.
Judge and conquer
All mankind in righteous war.

Thee let all mankind admire,
Object of our joy and dread!
Flame Thine eyes with heavenly fire,
Many crowns upon Thy head.
But Thine essence
None, except Thyself, can read.

Yet we know our Mediator,
By the Father's grace bestowed;
Meanly clothed in human nature,
Thee we call the Word of God.
Flesh Thy garment,
Dipped in Thy own sacred blood.

Captain, God of our salvation,
Thou Who hast the wine press trod,
Borne the Almighty's indignation,
Quenched the fiercest wrath of God,
Take the kingdom,
Claim the purchase of Thy blood.

On Thy thigh and clothing written,
Show the world Thy heavenly Name,
That, with loving wonder smitten,
All may glorify the Lamb.
All adore Thee,
All the Lord of hosts proclaim.

Honor, glory, and salvation
To the Lord our God we give.
Power, and endless adoration,
Thou art worthy to receive.
Reign triumphant,
King of kings, forever live!

COME, THOU LONG EXPECTED JESUS

Come, thou long expected Jesus,
born to set thy people free;
from our fears and sins release us,
let us find our rest in thee.
Israel's strength and consolation,
hope of all the earth thou art;
dear desire of every nation,
joy of every longing heart.

Born thy people to deliver,
born a child and yet a King,
born to reign in us forever,
now thy gracious kingdom bring.

By thine own eternal spirit
rule in all our hearts alone;
by thine all sufficient merit,
raise us to thy glorious throne.

COME, YE WEARY SINNERS, COME

Come, ye weary sinners, come, all who groan beneath your load,
Jesus calls His wanderers home, hasten to your pardoning God!
Come, ye guilty spirits oppressed, answer to the Savior's call,
"Come, and I will give you rest. Come, and I will save you all."

Jesus, full of truth and love, we Thy kindest word obey;
Faithful let Thy mercies prove, take our load of guilt away;
Now we would on Thee rely, cast on Thee our every care,
To Thine arms of mercy fly, find our lasting quiet there.

Burdened with a world of grief, burdened with our sinful load,
Burdened with this unbelief, burdened with the wrath of God;
Lo! we come to Thee for ease, true and gracious as Thou art,
Now our groaning souls release, write forgiveness on our heart.

DEPTH OF MERCY

Depth of mercy! Can there be
Mercy still reserved for me?
Can my God His wrath forbear,
Me, the chief of sinners, spare?

I have long withstood His grace,
Long provoked Him to His face,
Would not hearken to His calls,
Grieved Him by a thousand falls.

I have spilt His precious blood,
Trampled on the Son of God,
Filled with pangs unspeakable,
I, who yet am not in hell!

I my Master have denied,
I afresh have crucified,
And profaned His hallowed Name,
Put Him to an open shame.

Whence to me this waste of love?
Ask my Advocate above!
See the cause in Jesus' face,
Now before the throne of grace.

Jesus, answer from above,
Is not all Thy nature love?
Wilt Thou not the wrong forget,
Permit me to kiss Thy feet?

If I rightly read Thy heart,
If Thou all compassion art,
Bow Thine ear, in mercy bow,
Pardon and accept me now.

Jesus speaks, and pleads His blood!
He disarms the wrath of God;
Now my Father's mercies move,
Justice lingers into love.

Kindled His relentings are,
Me He now delights to spare,
Cries, "How shall I give thee up?"
Lets the lifted thunder drop.

Lo! I still walk on the ground:
Lo! an Advocate is found:
"Hasten not to cut Him down,
Let this barren soul alone."

There for me the Savior stands,
Shows His wounds and spreads His hands.
God is love! I know, I feel;
Jesus weeps and loves me still.

Pity from Thine eye let fall,
By a look my soul recall;
Now the stone to flesh convert,
Cast a look, and break my heart.

Now incline me to repent,
Let me now my sins lament,

Now my foul revolt deplore,
Weep, believe, and sin no more.

ETERNAL SON, ETERNAL LOVE

Eternal Son, eternal Love,
Take to Thyself Thy mighty power;
Let all earth's sons Thy mercy prove;
Let all Thy saving grace adore.

The triumphs of Thy love display;
In every heart reign Thou alone;
Till all Thy foes confess Thy sway,
And glory ends what grace began.

Spirit of grace with health and power,
Fountain of light and love below,
Abroad Thy healing influence shower,
O'er all the nations let it flow.

Inflame our hearts with perfect love;
In us the work of faith fulfill,
So not Heav'n's host shall swifter move
Than we on earth, to do Thy will.

FATHER OF JESUS CHRIST, MY LORD

Father of Jesus Christ, my Lord,
My Savior and my Head;
I trust in Thee, Whose powerful Word
Hath raised Him from the dead.

I hope, against all human hope,
Self desperate, I believe;
Thy quickening Word shall raise me up,
Thou shalt Thy Spirit give.

To Thee the glory of Thy power
And faithfulness I give;
I shall in Christ, at that glad hour,
And Christ in me shall live.

Faith, mighty faith, the promise sees,

And looks to that alone;
Laughs at impossibilities,
And cries, "It shall be done!"

FATHER, GOD, WE GLORIFY

Father, God, we glorify
Thy love to Adam's seed;
Love that gave Thy Son to die,
And raised Him from the dead:
Him, for our offenses slain,
That we all might pardon find,
Thou hast brought to life again,
The Savior of mankind.

By Thy own right hand of power
Thou hast exalted Him,
Sent the mighty Conqueror
Thy people to redeem:
King of Saints, and Prince of Peace,
Him Thou hast for sinners giv'n,
Sinners from their sins to bless,
And lift them up to Heav'n.

Father, God, to us impart
The gift unspeakable;
Now in every waiting heart
Thy glorious Son reveal:
Quickened with our living Lord,
Let us in Thy Spirit rise,
Rise to all Thy life restored,
And bless Thee in the skies.

FATHER, I STRETCH MY HANDS TO THEE

Father, I stretch my hands to Thee,
No other help I know;
If Thou withdraw Thyself from me,
Ah! whither shall I go?

What did Thine only Son endure,
Before I drew my breath!
What pain, what labor, to secure

My soul from endless death!

Surely Thou canst not let me die;
O speak, and I shall live;
And here I will unwearied lie,
Till Thou Thy Spirit give.

Author of faith! to Thee I lift
My weary, longing eyes:
O let me now receive that gift!
My soul without it dies.

FATHER, IN WHOM WE LIVE

Father, in Whom we live, in Whom we are and move,
The glory, power and praise receive for Thy creating love.
Let all the angel throng give thanks to God on high,
While earth repeats the joyful song and echoes to the sky.

Incarnate Deity, let all the ransomed race
Render in thanks their lives to Thee for Thy redeeming grace.
The grace to sinners showed ye heavenly choirs proclaim,
And cry "Salvation to our God, salvation to the Lamb!"

Spirit of Holiness, let all Thy saints adore
Thy sacred energy, and bless Thine heart renewing power.
Not angel tongues can tell Thy love's ecstatic height,
The glorious joy unspeakable the beatific sight.

Eternal, Triune God, let all the hosts above,
Let all on earth below record and dwell upon Thy love.
When heaven and earth are fled before Thy glorious face,
Sing all the saints Thy love hath made Thine everlasting praise.

FATHER, SON AND HOLY GHOST

Father, Son, and Holy Ghost,
In solemn power come down!
Present with Thy heavenly host,
Thine ordinance to crown:
See a sinful worm of earth!
Bless to him the cleansing flood,
Plunge him, by a second birth,

Into the depths of God.

Let the promised inward grace
Accompany the sign;
On his new-born soul impress
The character divine;
Father, all Thy Name reveal!
Jesus, all Thy Name impart!
Holy Ghost, renew, and dwell
For ever in his heart!

FATHER, WHOSE EVERLASTING LOVE

Father, Whose everlasting love
Thy only Son for sinners gave,
Whose grace to all did freely move,
And sent Him down the world to save;

Help us Thy mercy to extol,
Immense, unfathomed, unconfined;
To praise the Lamb who died for all,
The general Savior of mankind.

Thy undistinguishing regard
Was cast on Adam's fallen race;
For all Thou hast in Christ prepared
Sufficient, sovereign, saving grace.

The world He suffered to redeem;
For all He hath the atonement made;
For those that will not come to Him
The ransom of His life was paid.

Why then, Thou universal Love,
Should any of Thy grace despair?
To all, to all, Thy bowels move,
But straitened in our own we are.

Arise, O God, maintain Thy cause!
The fullness of the Gentiles call;
Lift up the standard of Thy cross,
And all shall own Thou diedst for all.

FOREVER HERE MY REST SHALL BE

Forever here my rest shall be,
Close to Thy bleeding side;
This all my hope, and all my plea,
For me the Savior died!

My dying Savior, and my God,
Fountain for guilt and sin,
Sprinkle me ever with Thy blood,
And cleanse, and keep me clean.

Wash me, and make me thus Thine own,
Wash me, and mine Thou art,
Wash me, but not my feet alone,
My hands, my head, my heart.

The atonement of Thy blood apply,
Till faith to sight improve,
Till hope in full fruition die,
And all my soul be love.

I do believe, I now believe,
That Jesus died for me;
And through His blood, His precious blood,
I shall from sin be free.

PART IV. FORTH IN THY NAME, O LORD

FORTH IN THY NAME, O LORD

Forth in Thy Name, O Lord, I go,
My daily labor to pursue;
Thee, only Thee, resolved to know
In all I think or speak or do.

The task Thy wisdom hath assigned,
O let me cheerfully fulfill;
In all my works Thy presence find,
And prove Thy good and perfect will.

Preserve me from my calling's snare,
And hide my simple heart above,
Above the thorns of choking care,
The gilded baits of worldly love.

Thee may I set at my right hand,
Whose eyes mine inmost substance see,
And labor on at Thy command,
And offer all my works to Thee.

Give me to bear Thy easy yoke,
And every moment watch and pray,
And still to things eternal look,
And hasten to Thy glorious day.

For Thee delightfully employ

Whate'er Thy bounteous grace
And run my course with even
And closely walk with Thee to

GENTLE JESUS, MEEK AI

Lamb of God, I look to The
Thou shalt my Example be;
Thou art gentle, meek, and r
Thou wast once a little chil

Lord, I would be as Thou
Give me Thine obedient h
Thou art pitiful and kind,
Let me have Thy loving mind.

Let me, above all, fulfill
God my heav'nly Father's will;
Never His good Spirit grieve;
Only to His glory live.

GIVE ME THE FAITH WHICH CAN REMOVE

Give me the faith which can remove
And sink the mountain to a plain;
Give me the childlike praying love,
Which longs to build Thy house again;
Thy love, let it my heart overpower,
And all my simple soul devour.

I want an even strong desire,
I want a calmly fervent zeal,
To save poor souls out of the fire,
To snatch them from the verge of hell,
And turn them to a pardoning God,
And quench the brands in Jesus' blood.

I would the precious time redeem,
And longer live for this alone,
To spend and to be spent for them
Who have not yet my Saviour known;
Fully on these my mission prove,
And only breathe, to breathe Thy love.

My talents, gifts, and graces, Lord,
Into Thy blessed hands receive;
And let me live to preach Thy Word,
And let me to Thy glory live;
My every sacred moment spend
In publishing the sinner's Friend.

Enlarge, inflame, and fill my heart
With boundless charity divine,
So shall I all strength exert,
And love them with a zeal like Thine,
And lead them to Thy open side,
The sheep for whom their Shepherd died.

Charles Wesley's original first stanza:

O that I was as heretofore
When first sent forth in Jesu's Name.
I rush'd thro' every open Door,
And cried to All, 'Behold the Lamb!'
Seiz'd the poor trembling Slaves of Sin,
And forc'd the Outcasts to come in.

GLORY BE TO GOD ON HIGH

Glory be to God on high,
God Whose glory fills the skies;
Peace on earth to man forgiv'n,
Man, the well beloved of Heav'n.

Sovereign Father, heavenly King,
Thee we now presume to sing;
Glad, Thine attributes confess,
Glorious all, and numberless.

Hail, by all Thy works adored!
Hail, the everlasting Lord!
Thee with thankful hearts we prove
God of power, and God of love.

Christ our Lord and God we own,
Christ, the Father's only Son,

Lamb of God for sinners slain,
Savior of offending man.

Bow Thine ear, in mercy bow,
Hear, the world's atonement, Thou!
Jesus, in Thy Name we pray,
Take, O take our sins away!

Powerful Advocate with God,
Justify us by Thy blood;
Bow Thine ear, in mercy bow,
Hear, the world's atonement, Thou!

Hear, for Thou, O Christ, alone
Art with God the Father One,
One the Holy Ghost with Thee,
One supreme, eternal Three.

GOD IS GONE UP ON HIGH

God is gone up on high,
With a triumphant noise;
The clarions of the sky
Proclaim the angelic joys!
Join all on earth, rejoice and sing;
Glory ascribe to glory's King.

God in the flesh below,
For us He reigns above:
Let all the nations know
Our Jesu's conquering love!
Join all on earth, rejoice and sing;
Glory ascribe to glory's King.

All power to our great Lord
Is by the Father given;
By angel hosts adored,
He reigns supreme in Heav'n:
Join all on earth, rejoice and sing;
Glory ascribe to glory's King.

High on His holy seat
He bears the righteous sway;

His foes beneath His feet
Shall sink and die away:
Join all on earth, rejoice and sing;
Glory ascribe to glory's King.

His foes and ours are one,
Satan, the world, and sin;
But He shall tread them down.
And bring His kingdom in:
Join all on earth, rejoice and sing;
Glory ascribe to glory's King.

Till all the earth, renewed
In righteousness divine,
With all the hosts of God
In one great chorus join,
Join all on earth, rejoice and sing;
Glory ascribe to glory's King

GOD OF ALL POWER AND TRUTH AND GRACE

God of all power, and truth, and grace,
Which shall from age to age endure,
Whose Word, when Heaven and earth shall pass,
Remains and stands for ever sure;

That I Thy mercy may proclaim,
That all mankind Thy truth may see,
Hallow Thy great and glorious Name,
And perfect holiness in me.

Thy sanctifying Spirit pour,
To quench my thirst, and make me clean;
Now, Father, let the gracious shower
Descend, and make me pure from sin.

Purge me from every sinful blot;
My idols all be cast aside;
Cleanse me from every sinful thought,
From all the filth of self and pride.

Give me a new, a perfect heart,
From doubt, and fear, and sorrow free;

The mind which was in Christ impart,
And let my spirit cleave to Thee.

O take this heart of stone away!
Thy sway it doth not, cannot own;
In me no longer let it stay,
O take away this heart of stone!

O that I now, from sin released,
Thy Word may to the utmost prove,
Enter into the promised rest,
The Canaan of Thy perfect love!

GOD ONLY WISE, AND GREAT, AND STRONG

God only wise, and great, and strong,
Hath made the orbs to run their race:
Knowledge and might to God belong,
Honor, and majesty, and praise.

Jehovah is unchangeable,
His ways and thoughts are not as ours;
He cheers the languid souls that fail;
And quickens all their drooping powers.

Gently He lifts the fallen up,
He gives them faith, and faith's increase,
Revives their feeble, dying hope,
And fills with love, and joy and peace.

Blasted, the vigor of the young
Shall fade, and suddenly decay;
The bold, and confident and strong,
Shall fear, despair, and die away.

But they who wait upon the Lord
Shall surely find His promise true,
Receive the quickening powerful Word,
And, born of God, their strength renew.

Their willing souls, from sin set free,
Shall swiftly in His statues move,
Shall walk in glorious liberty

Shall fly upon the wings of love.

GOOD THOU ART, AND GOOD THOU DOST

Good Thou art, and good Thou dost,
Thy mercies reach to all,
Chiefly those who on Thee trust,
And for Thy mercy call;
New they every morning are;
As fathers when their children cry,
Us Thou dost in pity spare,
And all our wants supply.

Mercy o'er Thy works presides;
Thy providence displayed
Still preserves, and still provides
For all Thy hands have made;
Keeps, with most distinguished care,
The man who on Thy love depends;
Watches every numbered hair,
And all his steps attends.

Who can sound the depths unknown
Of Thy redeeming grace?
Grace that gave Thine only Son
To save a ruined race!
Millions of transgressors poor
Thou hast for Jesus' sake forgiven,
Made them of Thy favor sure,
And snatched from hell to Heaven.

Millions more Thou ready art
To save, and to forgive;
Every soul and every heart
Of man Thou wouldst receive:
Father, now accept of mine,
Which now, through Christ, I offer Thee;
Tell me now, in love divine,
That Thou hast pardoned me!

HAIL THE DAY THAT SEES HIM RISE

Hail the day that sees Him rise, Alleluia!

To His throne above the skies, Alleluia!
Christ, awhile to mortals given, Alleluia!
Reascends His native heaven, Alleluia!

There the glorious triumph waits, Alleluia!
Lift your heads, eternal gates, Alleluia!
Christ hath conquered death and sin, Alleluia!
Take the King of glory in, Alleluia!

Circled round with angel powers, Alleluia!
Their triumphant Lord, and ours, Alleluia!
Conqueror over death and sin, Alleluia!
"Take the King of glory in! Alleluia!"

Him though highest Heav'n receives, Alleluia!
Still He loves the earth He leaves, Alleluia!
Though returning to His throne, Alleluia!
Still He calls mankind His own, Alleluia!

See! He lifts His hands above, Alleluia!
See! He shows the prints of love, Alleluia!
Hark! His gracious lips bestow, Alleluia!
Blessings on His church below, Alleluia!

Still for us His death He pleads, Alleluia!
Prevalent He intercedes, Alleluia!
Near Himself prepares our place, Alleluia!
Harbinger of human race, Alleluia!

Master, (will we ever say), Alleluia!
Taken from our head to day, Alleluia!
See Thy faithful servants, see, Alleluia!
Ever gazing up to Thee, Alleluia!

Grant, though parted from our sight, Alleluia!
Far above yon azure height, Alleluia!
Grant our hearts may thither rise, Alleluia!
Seeking Thee beyond the skies, Alleluia!

Ever upward let us move, Alleluia!
Wafted on the wings of love, Alleluia!
Looking when our Lord shall come, Alleluia!
Longing, gasping after home, Alleluia!

There we shall with Thee remain, Alleluia!
Partners of Thy endless reign, Alleluia!
There Thy face unclouded see, Alleluia!
Find our heaven of heavens in Thee, Alleluia!

HAPPY THE SOULS TO JESUS JOINED

Happy the souls to Jesus joined,
And saved by grace alone,
Walking in all His ways they find
Their heaven on earth begun.

The Church triumphant in Thy love,
Their mighty joys we know;
They sing the Lamb in hymns above,
And we in hymns below.

Thee in Thy glorious realm they praise,
And bow before Thy throne,
We in the kingdom of Thy grace:
The kingdoms are but one.

The holy to the holiest leads,
From thence our spirits rise,
And he that in Thy statutes treads
Shall meet Thee in the skies.

HARK A VOICE DIVIDES THE SKY

Hark! A voice divides the sky, happy are the faithful dead!
In the Lord who sweetly die, they from all their toils are freed;
Them the Spirit hath declared blessed, unutterably blessed;
Jesus is their great reward, Jesus is their endless rest.

Followed by their works, they go where their Head has gone before;
Reconciled by grace below, grace has opened mercy's door;
Justified through faith alone, here they knew their sins forgiven,
Here they laid their burden down, hallowed, and made fit for heaven.

Who can now lament the lot of a saint in Christ deceased?
Let the world, who know us not, call us hopeless and unblessed:
When from flesh the spirit freed hastens homeward to return,

Mortals cry, "A man is dead!" Angels sing, "A child is born!"

Born into the world above, they our happy brother greet,
Bear him to the throne of love, place him at the Savior's feet;
Jesus smiles, and says, "Well done, good and faithful servant thou;
Enter, and receive thy crown, reign with Me triumphant now."

Angels catch the approving sound, bow, and bless the just award;
Hail the heir with glory crowned, now rejoicing with his Lord:
Fuller joys ordained to know, waiting for the general doom,
When the archangel's trump shall blow, "Rise, ye dead, to judgment
come

HARK! THE HERALD ANGELS SING

Hark! the herald angels sing
Glory to the new-born King!
Peace on earth and mercy mild,
God and sinners reconciled.

Joyful all ye nations rise,
Join the triumph of the skies,
With the angelic host proclaim
Christ is born in Bethlehem!

Hail the heaven-born Prince of Peace!
Hail the Sun of Righteousness!
Light and life to all he brings,
Risen with healing in his wings.

Mild, he lays his glory by;
Born, that man no more may die,
Born to raise the sons of earth,
Born to give them second birth.

HE COMES, HE COMES, THE JUDGE SEVERE

He comes! He comes! the Judge severe!
The seventh trumpet speaks Him near;
His lightnings flash, His thunders roll;
How welcome to the faithful soul!

From Heav'n angelic voices sound;

See the almighty Jesus crowned,
Girt with omnipotence and grace!
And glory decks the Savior's face.

Descending on His great white throne,
He claims the kingdoms for His own;
The kingdoms all obey His Word,
And hail Him their triumphant Lord.

Shout, all the people of the sky,
And all the saints of the Most High;
Our Lord, Who now His right obtains,
Forever and forever reigns.

HEAD OF THY CHURCH TRIUMPHANT

Head of Thy Church triumphant,
We joyfully adore Thee;
Till Thou appear, Thy members here
Shall sing like those in glory.
We lift our hearts and voices
With blest anticipation,
And cry aloud, and give to God
The praise of our salvation.

While in affliction's furnace,
And passing through the fire,
Thy love we praise, which knows our days,
And ever brings us nigher.
We clap our hands exulting
In Thine almighty favor;
The love divine which made us Thine
Shall keep us Thine for ever.

Thou dost conduct Thy people
Through torrents of temptation,
Nor will we fear, while Thou art near,
The fire of tribulation.
The world with sin and Satan
In vain our march opposes,
Through Thee we shall break through them all,
And sing the song of Moses.

By faith we see the glory
To which Thou shalt restore us,
The cross despise for that high prize
Which Thou hast set before us.
And if Thou count us worthy,
We each, as dying Stephen,
Shall see Thee stand at God's right hand,
To take us up to Heaven.

HEAD OF THY CHURCH, WHOSE SPIRIT FILLS

Head of Thy church, whose Spirit fills
And flows through every faithful soul,
Unites in mystic love, and seals
Them one, and sanctifies the whole;

"Come, Lord," Thy glorious Spirit cries,
And souls beneath the altar groan;
"Come, Lord," the bride on earth replies,
"And perfect all our souls in one."

Pour out the promised gift on all,
Answer the universal "Come!"
The fullness of the Gentiles call,
And take thine ancient people home.

To Thee let all the nations flow,
Let all obey the Gospel word;
Let all their bleeding Savior know,
Filled with the glory of the Lord.

O for Thy truth and mercy's sake
The purchase of Thy passion claim!
Thine heritage the Gentiles take,
And cause the world to know Thy Name

HEARKEN TO THE SOLEMN VOICE

Hearken to the solemn voice, the awful midnight cry;
Waiting souls, rejoice, rejoice, and see the Bridegroom nigh;
Lo! He comes to keep His Word, light and joy His looks impart;
Go ye forth to meet your Lord, and meet Him in your heart.

Ye who faint beneath the load of sin, your heads lift up;
See your great redeeming God, He comes, and bids you hope:
In the midnight of your grief, Jesus doth His mourners cheer;
Lo! He brings you sure relief; believe, and feel Him here.

Ye whose loins are girt, stand forth! Whose lamps are burning bright,
Worthy, in your Savior's worth, to walk with Him in white:
Jesus bids your hearts be clean, bids you all His promise prove;
Jesus comes to cast out sin, and perfect you in love.

Wait we all in patient hope, till Christ, the Judge, shall come,
We shall soon be all caught up to meet the general doom:
In an hour to us unknown, as a thief in deepest night,
Christ shall suddenly come down, with all His saints in light.

Happy he whom Christ shall find watching to see Him come;
Him the Judge of all mankind shall bear triumphant home:
Who can answer to His Word? Which of you dares meet His day?
"Rise, and come to judgment!"—Lord, we rise, and come away.

HEAVENLY FATHER, SOVEREIGN LORD

Heavenly Father, sovereign Lord,
Ever faithful to Thy word,
Humbly we our seal set to,
Testify that Thou art true.
Lo! for us the wilds are glad,
All in cheerful green arrayed,
Opening sweets they all disclose,
Bud and blossom as the rose.

Hark! the wastes have found a voice,
Lonely deserts now rejoice,
Gladsome hallelujahs sing,
All around with praises ring.
Lo! abundantly they bloom,
Lebanon is hither come,
Carmel's stores the heavens dispense,
Sharon's fertile excellence.

See, these barren souls of ours
Bloom, and put forth fruits and flowers,
Flowers of Eden, fruits of grace,

Peace, and joy, and righteousness.
We behold (the abjects we!)
Christ, the incarnate Deity,
Christ, in whom Thy glories shine,
Excellence of strength divine.

Ye that tremble at his frown,
He shall lift your hands cast down;
Christ, who all your weakness sees,
He shall prop your feeble knees.
Ye of fearful hearts, be strong;
Jesus will not tarry long;
Fear not lest his truth should fail,
Jesus is unchangeable.

God, your God, shall surely come,
Quell your foes, and seal their doom,
He shall come and save you too;
We, O Lord, have found thee true!
Blind we were, but now we see,
Deaf; we hearken now to thee,
Dumb, for thee our tongues employ,
Lame, and, lo! we leap for joy.

Faint we were, and parched with drought,
Water at Thy word gushed out,
Streams of grace our thirst repress,
Starting from the wilderness;
Still we gasp Thy grace to know,
Here for ever let it flow,
Make the thirsty land a pool;
Fix the Spirit in our soul.

HOLY AS THOU, O LORD, IS NONE

Holy as Thou, O Lord, is none;
Thy holiness is all Thine own;
A drop of that unbounded sea
Is ours—a drop derived from Thee.

And when Thy purity we share,
Thine only glory we declare;
And, humbled into nothing, own,

Holy and pure is God alone.

Sole, self-existing God and Lord,
By all Thy heav'nly hosts adored,
Let all on earth bow down to Thee,
And own Thy peerless majesty.

Thy power unparalleled confess,
Established on the Rock of peace;
The Rock that never shall remove,
The Rock of pure, almighty, love.

HOLY, HOLY, LORD

Holy, holy, holy Lord,
God the Father, and the Word,
God the Comforter, receive
Blessings more than we can give!
Mixed with those beyond the sky,
Chanters to the Lord Most High,
We our hearts and voices raise,
Echoing Thy eternal praise.

One, inexplicably Three,
Three, in simplest Unity,
God, incline Thy gracious ear,
Us, Thy lisping creatures, hear!
Thee while man, the earth-born, sings,
Angels shrink within their wings;
Prostrate seraphim above
Breathe unutterable love.

Happy they who never rest,
With Thy heavenly presence blest!
They the heights of glory see,
Sound the depths of Deity.
Fain with them our souls would vie,
Sink as low, and mount as high;
Fall o'erwhelmed with love, or soar,
Shout, or silently adore.

HOW CAN WE SINNERS KNOW

How can we sinners know
our sins on earth forgiven?
How can my gracious Savior show
my name inscribed in heaven?

What we have felt and seen,
with confidence we tell,
and publish to the ends of earth
the signs infallible.

We who in Christ believe
that he for us hath died,
we all his unknown peace receive
and feel his blood applied.

We by his Spirit prove
and know the things of God,
the things which freely doth impart
and signs us with his cross.

The meek and lowly heart
that in our Savior was,
to us that Spirit doth impart
and signs us with his cross.

Our nature's turned, our mind
transformed in all its powers,
and both the witnesses are joined,
the Spirit of God with ours.

PART V. I KNOW THAT MY REDEEMER LIVES

I KNOW THAT MY REDEEMER LIVES

I know that my Redeemer lives,
And ever prays for me;
A token of his love he gives,
A pledge of liberty.

I find him lifting up my head,
He brings salvation near,
His presence makes me free indeed,
And he will soon appear.

He wills that I should holy be,
What can withstand his will?
The counsel of his grace in me
He surely shall fulfil.

Jesus, I hang upon thy word;
I steadfastly believe
Thou wilt return and claim me, Lord
And to thyself receive,

Joyful in hope, my spirit soars
To meet thee from above,
Thy goodness thankfully adores;
And sure I taste thy love.

Thy love I soon expect to find,

In all its depth and height;
To comprehend the Eternal Mind,
And grasp the Infinite.

When God is mine and I am his,
Of paradise possest,
I taste unutterable bliss,
And everlasting rest.

The bliss of those that fully dwell,
Fully in thee believe,
'Tis more than angel-tongues can tell,
Or angel-minds conceive.

Thou only know'st, who didst obtain,
And die to make it known;
The great salvation now explain,
And perfect us in one!

I WANT A PRINCIPLE WITHIN

I want a principle within
of watchful, godly fear,
a sensibility of sin,
a pain to feel it near.
I want the first approach to feel
of pride or wrong desire,
to catch the wandering of my will,
and quench the kindling fire.

From thee that I no more may stray,
no more thy goodness grieve,
grant me the filial awe, I pray,
the tender conscience give.
Quick as the apple of an eye,
O God, my conscience make;
awake my soul when sin is nigh,
and keep it still awake.

Almighty God of truth and love,
to me thy power impart;
the mountain from my soul remove,
the hardness from my heart.

O may the least omission pain
my reawakened soul,
and drive me to that blood again,
which makes the wounded whole.

IF DEATH MY FRIEND AND ME DIVIDE

If death my friend and me divide,
Thou dost not, Lord, my sorrow chide,
Or frown my tears to see;
Restrained from passionate excess,
Thou bidst me mourn in calm distress
For them that rest in Thee.

I feel a strong immortal hope,
Which bears my mournful spirit up
Beneath its mountain load;
Redeemed from death, and grief, and pain,
I soon shall find my friend again
Within the arms of God.

Pass a few fleeting moments more
And death the blessing shall restore
Which death has snatched away;
For me Thou wilt the summons send,
And give me back my parted friend
In that eternal day.

JESUS THE NAME HIGH OVER ALL

Jesus! the name high over all,
in hell or earth or sky;
angels and mortals prostrate fall,
and devils fear and fly.

Jesus! the name to sinners dear,
the name to sinners given;
it scatters all their guilty fear,
it turns their hell to heaven.

O that the world might taste and see
the riches of his grace!
The arms of love that compass me

would all the world embrace.

Thee I shall constantly proclaim,
though earth and hell oppose;
bold to confess thy glorious name
before a world of foes.

His only righteousness I show,
his saving truth proclaim;
'tis all my business here below
to cry, "Behold the Lamb!"

Happy, if with my latest breath
I may but gasp his name,
preach him to all and cry in death,
"Behold, behold the Lamb!"

JESUS, LORD, WE LOOK TO THEE

Jesus, Lord, we look to thee;
let us in thy name agree;
show thyself the Prince of Peace,
bid our strife forever cease.

By thy reconciling love
every stumbling block remove;
each to each unite, endear;
come, and spread thy banner here.

Make us of one heart and mind,
gentle, courteous, and kind,
lowly, meek, in thought and word,
altogether like our Lord.

Let us for each other care,
each the other's burdens bear;
to thy church the pattern give,
show how true believers live.

Free from anger and from pride,
let us thus in God abide;
all the depths of love express,
all the heights of holiness.

Let us then with joy remove
to the family above;
on the wings of angels fly,
show how true believers die.

JESUS, LOVER OF MY SOUL

Jesus, lover of my soul,
let me to thy bosom fly,
while the nearer waters roll,
while the tempest still is high.
Hide me, O my Savior, hide,
till the storm of life is past;
safe into the haven guide;
O receive my soul at last.

Other refuge have I none,
hangs my helpless soul on thee;
leave, ah! leave me not alone,
still support and comfort me.
All my trust on thee is stayed,
all my help from thee I bring;
cover my defenseless head
with the shadow of thy wing.

Wilt Thou not regard my call?
Wilt Thou not accept my prayer?
Lo! I sink, I faint, I fall-
Lo! on Thee I cast my care;
Reach me out Thy gracious hand!
While I of Thy strength receive,
Hoping against hope I stand,
dying, and behold, I live.

Thou, O Christ, art all I want,
more than all in thee I find;
raise the fallen, cheer the faint,
heal the sick, and lead the blind.
Just and holy is thy name,
I am all unrighteousness;
false and full of sin I am;
thou art full of truth and grace.

Plenteous grace with thee is found,
grace to cover all my sin;
let the healing streams abound,
make and keep me pure within.
Thou of life the fountain art,
freely let me take of thee;
spring thou up within my heart;
rise to all eternity.

JESUS, THE SINNER'S FRIEND

Jesus, the sinner's Friend, to thee,
Lost and undone, for aid I flee,
Weary of earth, myself, and sin:
Open Thine arms, and take me in.

Pity and save my ruined soul;
'Tis Thou alone canst make me whole;
Dark, 'til in me Thine image shine,
And lost, I am, 'til Thou art mine.

At last I own it cannot be
That I should fit myself for Thee:
Here, then, to Thee I all resign;
Thine is the work, and only Thine.

What can I say Thy grace to move?
Lord, I am sin, but Thou art love;
I give up every plea beside--
Lord, I am lost, but Thou hast died

JESUS, THINE ALL-VICTORIOUS LOVE

Jesus, thine all victorious love
shed in my heart abroad;
then shall my feet no longer rove,
rooted and fixed in God.

O that in me the sacred fire
might now begin to glow;
burn up the dross of base desire
and make the mountains flow!

O that it now from heaven might fall
and all my sins consume!
Come, Holy Ghost, for thee I call,
Spirit of burning, come!

Refining fire, go through my heart,
illuminate my soul;
scatter thy life through every part
and sanctify the whole.

JESUS, UNITED BY THY GRACE

Jesus, united by thy grace
and each to each endeared,
with confidence we seek thy face
and know our prayer is heard.

Help us to help each other, Lord,
each other's cross to bear;
let all their friendly aid afford,
and feel each other's care.

Up unto thee, our living Head,
let us in all things grow;
till thou hast made us free
indeed and spotless here below.

Touched by the lodestone of thy love,
let all our hearts agree,
and ever toward each other move,
and ever move toward thee.

To thee, inseparably joined,
let all our spirits cleave;
O may we all the loving mind
that was in thee receive.

This is the bond of perfectness,
thy spotless charity;
O let us, still we pray,
possess the mind that was in thee.

LET US PLEAD FOR FAITH ALONE

Let us plead for faith alone,
faith which by our works is shown;
God it is who justifies,
only faith the grace applies.

Active faith that lives within,
conquers hell and death and sin,
hallows whom it first made whole,
forms the Savior in the soul.

Let us for this faith contend,
sure salvation is the end;
heaven already is begun,
everlasting life is won.

Only let us persevere
till we see our Lord appear,
never from the Rock remove,
saved by faith which works by love.

LO, HE COMES WITH CLOUDS DESCENDING

Lo! He comes with clouds descending,
Once for favored sinners slain;
Thousand thousand saints attending,
Swell the triumph of His train:
Hallelujah! Hallelujah! Hallelujah!
God appears on earth to reign.

Every eye shall now behold Him
Robed in dreadful majesty;
Those who set at naught and sold Him,
Pierced and nailed Him to the tree,
Deeply wailing, deeply wailing, deeply wailing,
Shall the true Messiah see.

Every island, sea, and mountain,
Heav'n and earth, shall flee away;
All who hate Him must, confounded,
Hear the trump proclaim the day:
Come to judgment! Come to judgment! Come to judgment!

Come to judgment! Come away!

Now redemption, long expected,
See in solemn pomp appear;
All His saints, by man rejected,
Now shall meet Him in the air:
Hallelujah! Hallelujah! Hallelujah!
See the day of God appear!

Answer Thine own bride and Spirit,
Hasten, Lord, the general doom!
The new Heav'n and earth t'inherit,
Take Thy pining exiles home:
All creation, all creation, all creation,
Travails! groans! and bids Thee come!

The dear tokens of His passion
Still His dazzling body bears;
Cause of endless exultation
To His ransomed worshippers;
With what rapture, with what rapture, with what rapture
Gaze we on those glorious scars!

Yea, Amen! let all adore Thee,
High on Thine eternal throne;
Savior, take the power and glory,
Claim the kingdom for Thine own;
O come quickly! O come quickly! O come quickly!
Everlasting God, come down!

Alternately, the last two stanzas may be:

Now the Savior, long expected,
See, in solemn pomp appear;
All His saints, by man rejected,
Now shall meet Him in the air:
Alleluia, alleluia!

See the day of God appear.
Yea, amen! let all adore Thee,
High on Thine eternal throne;
Savior, take the pow'r and glory,
Claim the kingdom for Thine own:

O come quickly, O come quickly,
Alleluia! come, Lord, come!

LOVE DIVINE, ALL LOVES EXCELLING

Love divine, all loves excelling,
Joy of heaven, to earth come down;
fix in us thy humble dwelling;
all thy faithful mercies crown!
Jesus thou art all compassion,
pure, unbounded love thou art;
visit us with thy salvation;
enter every trembling heart.

Breathe, O breathe thy loving Spirit
into every troubled breast!
Let us all in thee inherit;
let us find that second rest.
Take away our bent to sinning;
Alpha and Omega be;
end of faith, as its beginning,
set our hearts at liberty.

Come, Almighty to deliver,
let us all thy life receive;
suddenly return and never,
nevermore thy temples leave.
Thee we would be always blessing,
serve thee as thy hosts above,
pray and praise thee without ceasing,
glory in thy perfect love.

Finish, then, thy new creation;
pure and spotless let us be.
Let us see thy great salvation
perfectly restored in thee;
changed from glory into glory,
till in heaven we take our place,
till we cast our crowns before thee,
lost in wonder, love, and praise.

MAKER, IN WHOM WE LIVE

Maker, in whom we live, in whom we are and move,
the glory, power, and praise receive for thy creating love.
Let all the angel throng give thanks to God on high,
while earth repeats the joyful song and echoes to the sky.

Incarnate Deity, let all the ransomed race
render in thanks their lives to thee for thy redeeming grace.
The grace to sinners showed ye heavenly choirs proclaim,
and cry, "Salvation to our God, salvation to the Lamb!"

Spirit of Holiness, let all thy saints adore
thy sacred energy, and bless thine heart-renewing power.
No angel tongues can tell thy love's ecstatic height,
the glorious joy unspeakable, the beatific sight.

Eternal, Triune God, let all the hosts above,
let all on earth below record and dwell upon thy love.
When heaven and earth are fled before thy glorious face,
sing all the saints thy love hath made thine everlasting praise.

MY HEART IS FIXED, O GOD

My heart is fixed, O God, my heart
Is fixed to triumph in thy grace:
(Awake, my lute, and bear a part)
My glory is to sing thy praise,
Till all thy nature I partake,
And bright in all thine image wake.

Thee will I praise among thine own;
Thee will I to the world extol,
And make thy truth and goodness known:
Thy goodness, Lord, is over all;
Thy truth and grace the heavens transcend;
Thy faithful mercies never end.

Be thou exalted, Lord, above
The highest name in earth or heaven;
Let angels sing thy glorious love,
And bless the name to sinners given;
All earth and heaven their King proclaim!
Bow every knee to Jesus' name!

O COME AND DWELL IN ME

O come and dwell in me,
Spirit of power within,
and bring the glorious liberty
from sorrow, fear, and sin.

Hasten the joyful day
which shall my sins consume,
when old things shall be done away,
and all things new become.

I want the witness, Lord,
that all I do is right,
according to thy mind and word,
well-pleasing in thy sight.

I ask no higher state;
indulge me but in this,
and soon or later then translate
to thine eternal bliss.

O FOR A HEART TO PRAISE MY GOD

O for a heart to praise my God,
a heart from sin set free,
a heart that always feels thy blood
so freely shed for me.

A heart resigned, submissive, meek,
my great Redeemer's throne,
where only Christ is heard to speak,
where Jesus reigns alone.

A humble, lowly, contrite heart,
believing, true, and clean,
which neither life nor death can part
from Christ who dwells within.

A heart in every thought renewed
and full of love divine,
perfect and right and pure and good,
a copy, Lord, of thine.

Thy nature, gracious Lord, impart;
come quickly from above;
write thy new name upon my heart,
thy new, best name of Love.

O FOR A THOUSAND TONGUES TO SING

Glory to God, and praise and love
Be ever, ever given,
By saints below and saints above,
The church in earth and heaven.

On this glad day the glorious Sun
Of Righteousness arose;
On my benighted soul He shone
And filled it with repose.

Sudden expired the legal strife,
'Twas then I ceased to grieve;
My second, real, living life
I then began to live.

Then with my heart I first believed,
Believed with faith divine,
Power with the Holy Ghost received
To call the Savior mine.

I felt my Lord's atoning blood
Close to my soul applied;
Me, me He loved, the Son of God,
For me, for me He died!

I found and owned His promise true,
Ascertained of my part,
My pardon passed in heaven I knew
When written on my heart.

O for a thousand tongues to sing
My great (orig. dear) Redeemer's praise,
The glories of my God and King,
The triumphs of his grace!

My gracious Master and my God,
Assist me to proclaim,
To spread through all the earth abroad
The honors of Thy name.

Jesus! The name that charms our fears,
That bids our sorrows cease;
'Tis music in the sinner's ears,
'Tis life, and health, and peace.

He breaks the power of canceled sin,
He sets the prisoner free;
His blood can make the foulest clean,
His blood availed for me.

He speaks, and, listening to his voice,
New life the dead receive,
The mournful, broken hearts rejoice,
The humble poor believe.

Hear Him, ye deaf, His praise, ye dumb,
Your loosened tongues employ;
Ye blind, behold your Savior come,
And leap, ye lame, for joy.

Look unto Him, ye nations, own
Your God, ye fallen race;
Look, and be saved through faith alone,
Be justified by grace.

See all your sins on Jesus laid:
The Lamb of God was slain,
His soul was once an offering made
For every soul of man.

Harlots and publicans and thieves
In holy triumph join!
Saved is the sinner that believes
From crimes as great as mine.

Murderers and all ye hellish crew
Ye sons of lust and pride,
Believe the Savior died for you;

For me the Savior died.

Awake from guilty nature's sleep,
And Christ shall give you light,
Cast all your sins into the deep,
And wash the Æthiop white.

With me, your chief, ye then shall know,
Shall feel your sins forgiven;
Anticipate your heaven below,
And own that love is heaven.

O LOVE DIVINE, WHAT HAST THOU DONE

O Love divine, what has thou done!
The immortal God hath died for me!
The Father's coeternal Son
bore all my sins upon the tree.
Th' immortal God for me hath died:
My Lord, my Love, is crucified!

Is crucified for me and you,
to bring us rebels back to God.
Believe, believe the record true,
ye all are bought with Jesus' blood.
Pardon for all flows from his side:
My Lord, my Love, is crucified!

Behold him, all ye that pass by,
the bleeding Prince of life and peace!
Come, sinners, see your Savior die,
and say, "Was ever grief like his?"
Come, feel with me his blood applied:
My Lord, my Love, is crucified

ALL GLORY TO OUR GRACIOUS LORD

All glory to our gracious Lord!
His love be by his church adored,
His love eternally the same!
His love let Aaron's sons confess,
His free and everlasting grace
Let all that fear the Lord proclaim.

The Lord I now can say is mine,
And, confident in strength divine,
Nor man, nor fiends, nor flesh I fear,
Jesus the Saviour takes my part,
And keeps the issues of my heart;
My helper is for ever near.

Righteous I am in him, and strong,
He is become my joyful song,
My Saviour and salvation too:
I triumph through his mighty grace,
And pure in heart shall see his face,
And rise in Christ a creature new.

The voice of joy, and love, and praise,
And thanks for his redeeming grace
Among the justified is found:
With songs that rival those above,
With shouts proclaiming Jesu's love,
Both day and night their tents resound.

The Lord's right hand hath wonders wrought
Above the reach of human thought,
The Lord's right hand exalted is;
We see it still stretched out to save;
The power of God in Christ we have,
And Jesus is the Prince of peace.

Open the gates of righteousness,
Receive me into Christ my peace,
That I his praises may record;
He is the Truth, the Life, the Way,
The portal of eternal day,
The gate of heaven is Christ my Lord.

Jesus is lifted up on high,
Whom man refused and doomed to die,
He is become the corner-stone;
Head of the church he lives and reigns,
His kingdom over all maintains,
High on his everlasting throne.

The Lord the amazing work hath wrought,
Hath from the dead our Shepherd brought,
Revived on the third glorious day:
This is the day our God hath made,
The day for sinners to be glad
In him who bears their sins away.

Thee, Lord, with joyful lips we praise,
O send us now thy saving grace,
Make this the acceptable hour:
Our hearts would now receive thee in;
Enter, and make an end of sin,
And bless us with the perfect power.

Bless us, that we may call thee blest,
Sent down from heaven to give us rest,
Thy gracious Father to proclaim
His sinless nature to impart,
In every new, believing heart
To manifest his glorious name.

God is the Lord that shows us light,
Then let us render him his right,
The offerings of a thankful mind;
Present our living sacrifice,
And to his cross in closest ties
With cords of love our Spirit bind.

Thou art my God, and thee I praise,
Thou art my God, I sing thy grace.
And call mankind to extol thy name:
All glory to our gracious Lord!
His name be praised, his love adored,
Through all eternity the same!

PART VI. O THOU WHO CAMEST FROM ABOVE

O THOU WHO CAMEST FROM ABOVE

O Thou who camest from above,
the pure celestial fire to impart
kindle a flame of sacred love
upon the mean altar of my heart.

There let it for thy glory burn
with inextinguishable blaze,
and trembling to its source return,
in humble prayer and fervent praise.

Jesus, confirm my heart's desire
to work and speak and think for thee;
still let me guard the holy fire,
and still stir up thy gift in me.

Ready for all thy perfect will,
my acts of faith and love repeat,
till death thy endless mercies seal,
and make my sacrifice complete.

PRAISE THE LORD WHO REIGNS ABOVE

Praise the Lord who reigns above
and keeps his court below;
praise the holy God of love
and all his greatness show;

praise him for his noble deeds,
praise him for his matchless power;
him from whom all good proceeds
let earth and heaven adore.

Celebrate th' eternal God
with harp and psaltery,
timbrels soft and cymbals loud
in this high praise agree;
praise with every tuneful string;
all the reach of heavenly art,
all the powers of music bring,
the music of the heart.

God, in whom they move and live,
let every creature sing,
glory to their Maker give,
and homage to their King.
Hallowed be thy name beneath,
as in heaven on earth adored;
praise the Lord in every breath,
let all things praise the Lord.

REJOICE, THE LORD IS KING

Rejoice, the Lord is King!
Your Lord and King adore;
mortals, give thanks and sing,
and triumph evermore.
Lift up your heart,
lift up your voice; rejoice;
again I say, rejoice.

Jesus the Savior reigns,
the God of truth and love;
when he had purged our stains,
he took his seat above.
Lift up your heart,
lift up your voice; rejoice,
again I say, rejoice.

His kingdom cannot fail;
he rules o'er earth and heaven;

the keys of earth and hell
are to our Jesus given.
Lift up your heart,
lift up your voice; rejoice,
again I say, rejoice.

He sits at God's right hand
till all His foes submit,
and bow to His command,
and fall beneath His feet:
Lift up your heart,
lift up your voice; rejoice,
again I say, rejoice!

Rejoice in glorious hope!
Jesus the Judge shall come,
and take his servants up
to their eternal home.
We soon shall hear
th'archangel's voice; the trump of God
shall sound, rejoice!

SOLDIERS OF CHRIST, ARISE

Soldiers of Christ arise,
and put your armor on,
strong in the strength which God supplies
thru his eternal Son;
strong in the Lord of Hosts,
and in his mighty power,
who in the strength of Jesus trusts
is more than conqueror.

Stand then in his great might,
with all his strength endued,
but take to arm you for the fight
the panoply of God;
that having all things done,
and all your conflicts passed,
ye may o'ercome thru Christ alone
and stand entire at last.

Pray without ceasing, pray,

(your Captain gives the word)
his summons cheerfully obey
and call upon the Lord;
to God your every want
in instant prayer display,
pray always, pray and never faint,
pray, without ceasing pray.

From strength to strength go on,
wrestle and fight and pray,
tread all the powers of darkness down
and win the well-fought day.
Still let the Spirit cry
in all his soldiers, "Come!"
till Christ the Lord, descends from high
and takes the conquerors home.

SPIRIT OF FAITH, COME DOWN

Spirit of faith, come down,
reveal the things of God,
and make to us the Godhead known,
and witness with the blood.
'Tis thine the blood to apply
and give us eyes to see,
who did for every sinner die
hath surely died for me.

No one can truly say
that Jesus is the Lord,
unless thou take the veil away
and breathe the living Word.
Then, only then, we feel
our interest in his blood,
and cry with joy unspeakable,
"Thou art my Lord, my God!"

O that the word might know
the all atoning Lamb!
Spirit of faith, descend and show
the virtue of his name;
the grace which all may find,
the saving power, impart,

and testify to humankind,
and speak in every heart.

Inspire the living faith
(which whosoe'er receive,
the witness in themselves they have
and consciously believe),
the faith that conquers all,
and doth the mountain move,
and saves whoe'er on Jesus call,
and perfects them in love

THE GREAT ARCHANGEL'S TRUMP

The great archangel's trump shall sound,
While twice ten thousand thunders roar
Tear up the graves, and cleave the ground,
And make the greedy sea restore.

The greedy sea shall yield her dead,
The earth no more her slain conceal;
Sinners shall lift their guilty head,
And shrink to see a yawning hell.

But we, who now our Lord confess,
And faithful to the end endure,
Shall stand in Jesus' righteousness,
Stand, as the Rock of ages, sure.

We, while the stars from heaven shall fall,
And mountains are on mountains hurled,
Shall stand unmoved amidst them all,
And smile to see a burning world.

The earth, and all the works therein,
Dissolve, by raging flames destroyed,
While we survey the awful scene,
And mount above the fiery void.

By faith we now transcend the skies,
And on that ruined world look down;
By love above all height we rise,
And share the everlasting throne.

THOU HIDDEN SOURCE OF CALM REPOSE

Thou hidden source of calm repose,
thou all-sufficient love divine,
my help and refuge from my foes,
secure I am if thou art mine;
and lo! from sin and grief and shame
I hide me, Jesus, in thy name.

Thy mighty name salvation is,
and keeps my happy soul above,
comfort it brings, and power and peace,
and joy and everlasting love;
to me with thy dear name are given
pardon and holiness and heaven.

Jesus, my all in all thou art,
my rest in toil, my ease in pain,
the healing of my broken heart,
in war my peace, in loss my gain,
my smile beneath the tryrant's frown,
in shame my glory and my crown.

In want my plentiful supply,
in weakness my almighty power,
in bonds my perfect liberty,
my light in Satan's darkest hour,
my help and stay whene'er I call,
my life in death, my heaven, my all.

TIS FINISHED,THE MESSIAH DIES

'Tis finished! The Messiah dies,
Cut off for sins, but not His own:
Accomplished is the sacrifice,
The great redeeming work is done.
'Tis finished! all the debt is paid;
Justice divine is satisfied;
The grand and full atonement made;
God for a guilty world hath died.

The veil is rent in Christ alone;

The living way to Heaven is seen;
The middle wall is broken down,
And all mankind may enter in.
The types and figures are fulfilled;
Exacted is the legal pain;
The precious promises are sealed;
The spotless Lamb of God is slain.

The reign of sin and death is o'er,
And all may live from sin set free;
Satan hath lost his mortal power;
'Tis swallowed up in victory.
Saved from the legal curse I am,
My Savior hangs on yonder tree:
See there the meek, expiring Lamb!
'Tis finished! He expires for me.

Accepted in the Well-beloved,
And clothed in righteousness divine,
I see the bar to heaven removed;
And all Thy merits, Lord, are mine.
Death, hell, and sin are now subdued;
All grace is now to sinners given;
And lo, I plead the atoning blood,
And in Thy right I claim Thy Heaven!

YE SERVANTS OF GOD

Ye servants of God, your Master proclaim,
and publish abroad his wonderful name;
the name all-victorious of Jesus extol,
his kingdom is glorious and rules over all.

The waves of the sea have lift up their voice,
Sore troubled that we in Jesus rejoice;
The floods they are roaring, but Jesus is here;
While we are adoring, He always is near.

When devils engage, the billows arise,
And horribly rage, and threaten the skies:
Their fury shall never our steadfastness shock,
The weakest believer is built on a rock.

God ruleth on high, almighty to save,
and still he is nigh, his presence we have;
the great congregation his triumph shall sing,
ascribing salvation to Jesus, our King.

"Salvation to God, who sits on the throne!"
Let all cry aloud and honor the Son;
the praises of Jesus the angels proclaim,
fall down on their faces and worship the Lamb.

Then let us adore and give him his right,
all glory and power, all wisdom and might;
all honor and blessing with angels above,
and thanks never ceasing and infinite love

A FEW MORE YEARS SHALL ROLL

A few more years shall roll,
A few more seasons come;
And we shall be with those that rest,
Asleep within the tomb.

Then, O my Lord, prepared
My soul for that great day;
O wash me in thy precious blood,
And take my sins away!

A few more suns shall set
O'er these dark hills of time;
And we shall be where suns are not,
A far serener clime.

A few more storms shall beat
On this wild rocky shore;
And we shall be where tempests cease,
And surges swell no more.

A few more struggles here,
A few more partings o'er,
A few more toils, a few more tears,
And we shall weep no more.

A few more Sabbaths here

Shall cheer us on our way;
And we shall reach the endless rest,
The eternal Sabbath-day.

ABBA, FATHER, HEAR THY CHILD

Abba, Father, hear thy child,
Late in Jesus reconciled;
Hear, and all the graces shower,
All the joy, and peace, and power;
All my Saviour asks above,
All the life and heaven of love.

Lord, I will not let thee go
Till the blessing thou bestow:
Hear my Advocate divine;
Lo! To his my suit I join;
Joined to his, it cannot fail;
Bless me; for I will prevail.

Heavenly Father, Life divine,
Change my nature into thine;
Move, and spread throughout my soul,
Actuate, and fill the whole:
Be it I no longer now
Living in the flesh, but thou.

Holy Ghost, no more delay;
Come, and in thy temple stay:
Now thine inward witness bear,
Strong, and permanent, and clear:
Spring of life, thyself impart;
Rise eternal in my heart

ABRAHAM, WHEN SEVERELY TRIED

Abraham, when severely tried,
His faith by his obedience showed,
He with the harsh command complied,
And gave his Isaac back to God.

His son the father offered up,
Son of his age, his only son,

Object of all his joy and hope,
And less beloved than God alone.

O for a faith like his, that we
The bright example may pursue!
May gladly give up all to thee,
To whom our more than all is due.

Now, Lord, to thee our all we leave,
Our willing soul thy call obeys;
Pleasure, and wealth, and fame we give,
Freedom, and life to win thy grace.

Is there a thing than life more dear?
A thing from which we cannot part?
We can; we now rejoice to tear
The idol from our bleeding heart.

Jesus, accept our sacrifice;
All things for thee we count but loss,
Lo! at thy word our Isaac dies,
Dies on the altar of thy cross.

For what to thee, O Lord, we give,
A hundred-fold we here obtain;
And soon with thee shall all receive,
And loss shall be eternal gain.

AH TELL US NO MORE

Ah, tell us no more
The spirit and pow'r
Of Jesus, our God,
Is not to be found in this lifegiving Blood!

Did Jesus ordain
His supper in vain,
And furnish a feast
For none but His earliest servants to taste?

Nay, but this is His will
(We know it and feel),
That we should partake

The banquet for all He so freely did make.

In rapturous bliss
He bids us do this.
The joy it imparts
Hath witness'd His gracious design in our hearts.

AH WHITHER SHOULD I GO

Ah! whither should I go,
Burdened and sick and faint?
To whom should I my trouble show,
And pour out my complaint?
My Savior bids me come;
Ah! why do I delay?
He calls the weary sinner home,
And yet from Him I stay.

What is it keeps me back,
From which I cannot part,
Which will not let the Savior take
Possession of my heart?
Searcher of hearts, in mine
Thy trying power display;
Into its darkest corners shine,
And take the veil away.

I now believe in Thee,
Compassion reigns alone;
According to my faith, to me
O let it, Lord, be done!
In me is all the bar,
Which Thou wouldst fain remove;
Remove it, and I shall declare
That God is only love.

ALL GLORY TO GOD

All glory to God, and peace upon earth,
Be published abroad at Jesus' birth;
The forfeited favor of Heaven we find
Restored in the Savior and Friend of mankind.

Then let us behold Messias the Lord,
By prophets foretold, by angels adored;
Our God's incarnation with angels proclaim,
And publish salvation in Jesus' Name.

Our newly born King by faith we have seen
And joyfully sing His goodness to men,
That all men may wonder at what we impart,
And thankfully ponder His love in their heart.

What moved the Most High so greatly to stoop,
He comes from the sky our souls to lift up;
That sinners forgiven, might sinless return
To God and to Heaven; their Maker is born.

Immanuel's love let sinners confess,
Who comes from above, to bring us His peace;
Let every believer His mercy adore,
And praise Him forever, when time is no more.

ALL GLORY TO GOD IN THE SKY

All glory to God in the sky,
And peace upon earth be restored!
O Jesus, exalted on high,
Appear our omnipotent Lord:
Who meanly in Bethlehem born,
Didst stoop to redeem a lost race,
Once more to Thy creature return,
And reign in Thy kingdom of grace.

When Thou in our flesh didst appear,
All nature acknowledged Thy birth;
Arose the acceptable year,
And Heaven was opened on earth.
Receiving its Lord from above,
The world was united to bless
The Giver of concord and love,
The Prince and the Author of peace.

O wouldst Thou again be made known,
Again in Thy Spirit descend,
And set up in each of Thine own

A kingdom that never shall end!
Thou only art able to bless,
And make the glad nations obey,
And bid the dire enmity cease,
And bow the whole world to Thy sway.

Come then to Thy servants again,
Who long Thy appearing to know,
Thy quiet and peaceable reign,
In mercy establish below:
All sorrow before Thee shall fly,
And anger and hatred be o'er,
And envy and malice shall die,
And discord afflict us no more.

No horrid alarm of war
Shall break our eternal repose;
No sound of the trumpet is there,
Where Jesus' Spirit o'erflows:
Appeased by the charms of Thy grace
We all shall in amity join,
And kindly each other embrace,
And love with a passion like Thine.

ALL PRAISE TO HIM WHO DWELLS IN BLISS

All praise to Him Who dwells in bliss,
Who made both day and night;
Whose throne is darkness, in th'abyss
Of uncreated light.

Each thought and deed His piercing eyes
With strictest search survey;
The deepest shades no more disguise
Than the full blaze of day.

Whom Thou dost guard, O King of kings,
No evil shall molest;
Under the shadow of Thy wings,
Shall they securely rest.

Thy angels shall around their beds
Their constant stations keep;

Thy faith and truth shall shield their heads,
For Thou dost never sleep.

May we, with calm and sweet repose,
And heavenly thoughts refreshed,
Our eyelids with the morn's unclose,
And bless the Ever-blessed.

ALL PRAISE TO OUR REDEEMING LORD

All praise to our redeeming Lord,
Who joins us by His grace;
And bids us, each to each restored,
Together seek His face.

He bids us build each other up;
And, gathered into one,
To our high calling's glorious hope,
We hand in hand go on.

The gift which He on one bestows,
We all delight to prove;
The grace through every vessel flows,
In purest streams of love.

E'en now we think and speak the same,
And cordially agree;
Concentered all, through Jesus' Name,
In perfect harmony.

We all partake the joy of one;
The common peace we feel;
A peace to sensual minds unknown,
A joy unspeakable.

And if our fellowship below
In Jesus be so sweet,
What height of rapture shall we know
When round His throne we meet!

ALL PRAISE TO THE LAMB

All praise to the Lamb! Accepted I am,

Through faith in the Saviour's adorable name:
In him I confide, his blood is applied;
For me he hath suffered, for me he hath died.

Not a cloud doth arise, to darken my skies,
Or hide for a moment my Lord from mine eye:
In him I am blest, I lean on his breast
And lo! in his wounds I continue to rest.

ALL THANKS TO THE LAMB

All thanks to the Lamb, Who gives us to meet!
His love we proclaim, His praises repeat;
We own Him our Jesus, continually near
To pardon and bless us and perfect us here.

In Him we have peace, in Him we have power,
Preserved by His grace throughout the dark hour,
In all our temptation He keeps us to prove
His utmost salvation, His fullness of love.

Through pride and desire unhurt we have gone,
Through water and fire in Him we went on;
The world and the devil through Him we o'ercame,
Our Saviour from evil, for ever the same.

When we would have spurned His mercy and grace,
To Egypt returned, and fled from His face,
He hindered our flying (His goodness to show),
And stopped us by crying, "Will ye also go?"

O what shall we do our Saviour to love?
To make us anew, come, Lord, from above.
The fruit of Thy passion, Thy holiness give,
Give us the salvation of all that believe.

Pronounce the glad word, and bid us be free!
Ah! hast Thou not, Lord, a blessing for me?
The peace Thou hast given this moment impart,
And open Thy heaven of love in my heart.

Come, Jesus, and loose the stammerer's tongue,
And teach even us the spiritual song;

Let us without ceasing give thanks for Thy grace,
And glory, and blessing, and honour, and praise.

ALL WISE, ALL GOOD, ALMIGHTY LORD

All wise, all good, almighty Lord,
Jesus, by highest Heav'n adored,
Ere time its course began;
How did Thy glorious mercy stoop,
To take Thy fallen children up,
When Thou Thyself wert man?

Th'eternal God from Heav'n came down;
The King of glory dropped His crown
And veiled His majesty;
Emptied of all but love He came,
Jesus, I call Thee by the Name,
Thy pity bore for me.

O holy Child, still let Thy birth
Bring peace to us poor worms of earth,
And praise to God on high!
Come, Thou who didst my flesh assume;
Now to the abject sinner come,
And in a manger lie.

Didst Thou not in person join
The natures human and divine,
That God and man might be
Henceforth inseparably one?
Haste then and make Thy nature known
Incarnated in me.

In my weak, sinful flesh appear,
O God, be manifested here,
Peace, righteousness and joy;
Thy kingdom, Lord, set up within
My faithful heart; and all my sin,
The devil's work, destroy.

I long Thy coming to confess,
The mystic power of godliness,
The life divine to prove:

The fulness of Thy life to know,
Redeemed from all my sins below,
And perfected in love.

O Christ, my Hope, make known to me
The great, the glorious mystery
The hidden life impart;
Come, Thou Desire of nations, come,
Formed in a spotless virgin's womb,
A pure, believing heart.

Come quickly, dearest Lord, that I
May own, tho' Antichrist deny,
Thy incarnation's power:
May cry, a witness to my Lord,
"Come in my flesh is Christ the Word,
And I can sin no more!"

ALL YE THAT PASS BY

All ye that pass by,
To Jesus draw nigh:
To you is it nothing that Jesus should die?
Your ransom and peace,
Your surety He is:
Come, see if there ever was sorrow like His.

For what you have done
His blood must atone:
The Father hath punished for you His dear Son.
The Lord, in the day
Of His anger, did lay
Your sins on the Lamb, and He bore them away.

He answered for all:
O come at His call,
And low at His cross with astonishment fall!
But lift up your eyes
At Jesus' cries:
Impassive, He suffers; immortal, He dies.

He dies to atone
For sins not His own;

Your debt He hath paid, and your work He hath done.
Ye all may receive
The peace He did leave,
Who made intercession, "My Father, forgive!"

For you and for me
He prayed on the tree:
The prayer is accepted, the sinner is free.
That sinner am I,
Who on Jesus rely,
And come for the pardon God cannot deny.

My pardon I claim;
For a sinner I am,
A sinner believing in Jesus' Name.
He purchased the grace
Which now I embrace:
O Father, Thou know'st He hath died in my place.

His death is my plea;
My Advocate see,
And hear the blood speak that hath answered for me.
My ransom He was
When He bled on the cross;
And losing His life He hath carried my cause.

ALL YE THAT SEEK THE LORD WHO DIED

All ye that seek the Lord Who died,
Your God for sinners crucified,
Prevent the earliest dawn, and come
To worship at His sacred tomb.

Bring the sweet spices of your sighs,
Your contrite hearts, and streaming eyes,
Your sad complaints, and humble fears;
Come, and embalm Him with your tears.

While thus ye love your souls t'employ,
Your sorrow shall be turned to joy:
Now, let all your grief be o'er!
Believe, and ye shall weep no more.

An earthquake hath the cavern shook,
And burst the door, and rent the rock;
The Lord hath sent His angel down,
And he hath rolled away the stone.

As snow behold his garment white,
His countenance as lightning bright:
He sits, and waves a flaming sword,
And waits upon his rising Lord.

The third auspicious morn is come,
And calls your Savior from the tomb,
The bands of death are torn away,
The yawning tomb gives back its prey.

Could neither seal nor stone secure,
Nor men, nor devils make it sure?
The seal is broke, the stone cast by,
And all the powers of darkness fly.

The body breathes, and lifts His head,
The keepers sink, and fall as dead;
The dead restored to life appear,
The living quake, and die for fear.

No power a band of soldiers have
To keep one body in its grave:
Surely it no dead body was
That could the Roman eagles chase.

The Lord of Life is risen indeed,
To death delivered in your stead;
His rise proclaims your sins forgiv'n,
And show the living way to Heav'n.

Haste then, ye souls that first believe,
Who dare the Gospel-Word receive,
Your faith with joyful hearts confess,
Be bold, be Jesus' witnesses.

Go tell the followers of your Lord
Their Jesus is to life restored;
He lives, that they His life may find;

He lives, to quicken all mankind.

AMBASSADORS OF GOD

God, the offended God most high,
Ambassadors to rebels sends;
His messengers His place supply,
And Jesus begs us to be friends.

Us, in the stead of Christ, they pray,
Us, in the stead of God, entreat,
To cast our arms, our sins, away,
And find forgiveness at His feet.

Our God in Christ! Thine embassy,
And proffered mercy, we embrace;
And gladly reconciled to Thee,
Thy condescending goodness praise.

Poor debtors, by our Lord's request
A full acquittance we receive!
And criminals, with pardon blessed,
We, at our Judge's instance, live!

What are your works but sin and death
Thill thou thy quick'ning Spirit breathe;
Thou giv'st the power thy grace to move;
O wondrous grace! O boundless love!"

"Thou all our works in us hast wrought,
Our good is all divine;
The praise of every virtuous thought
And righteous word is thine."

Look unto him, ye nations; own
Your God, ye fallen race;
Look, and be saved through faith alone
Be justified by grace.

... Mercy and grace are thine alone,
And power and wisdom too;
Without the Spirit of thy Son
We nothing good can do
We cannot speak one useful word.
One holy thought conceive
Unless, in answer to our Lord,
Thyself the blessing give.

Wrestling Jacob

„I design plain truth for plain
people; therefore, of set purpose,
I abstain from all nice and
philosophical speculations, from
all perplexed and intricate
reasonings, unless in sometimes
citing the original scriptures."

John Wesley
(Wesleyana)

„Father, how wide thy glories shine!
Lord of the universe, –– and mine:
Thy goodness watches o'er the whole,
As all the world were lent one soul:
Yet keeps my every sacred hour,
As I remain'd thy single care!"

7129651R00066

Printed in Germany
by Amazon Distribution
GmbH, Leipzig